SCHOOL

OF

CALVARY

AND

THE PASSION FOR SOULS

SCHOOL

OF

CALVARY

AND

THE PASSION FOR SOULS

THE SCHOOL OF CALVARY

OR,

SHARING HIS SUFFERING

AND

THE PASSION FOR SOULS

J. H. Jowett, M.A.,D.D.

CCR
PUBLICATIONS

CHRIST CHURCH — RADFORD

THE SCHOOL OF CALVARY | AND | A PASSION FOR SOULS
OR SHARING HIS SUFFERING

This edition Copyright © 2014 by Christ Church — Radford
Author: J. H. Jowett, M.A.,D.D.

Published by CCR Publications
        a publishing ministry of Christ Church — Radford
        6226 University Park Drive
        Radford, VA 24141
        christchurchradford.org

This edition is a revision of the original edition printed by
James Clarke And Company, London, In 1911

Cover design and Interior design: Jon Green
Cover Illustration adapted from Gustave Doré Jesus in Garden of Gethsemane.
First Printing. 2014
Printed in the United States of America

Unless otherwise indicated, Scripture references are from the Holy Bible, King James
Version (KJV).

Please visit our website at:
christchurchradford.org

ISBN: 978-1-4948-7893-1

CONTENTS

J. H. Jowett
(August 25th, 1863 - 20 December 17th, 1923)

INTRODUCTION

A Portrait of J. H. Jowett

Dr. Jowett excels in what John Morley[1] in a fine phrase calls "the imaginative treatment of the common-place." His mind is a veritable storehouse of illustration and metaphor, drawn chiefly from the broad ways of nature. He delights in the homely illustration, and the triumph is that he makes it convey so much. If you walk with him along a country lane his eye is quick to detect the hidden mysteries of the countryside, but even quicker is his imagination to discern the analogy between the material happening and his own deeper philosophy of the soul. It is this broad sympathy with nature in her simpler moods and his remarkable gift of expressing his thoughts in a highly picturesque form which have contributed so largely to his popularity among all classes of the religious community.

In one respect Dr. Jowett's style is a return to simplicity, a protest against the artificiality of dogmatic theology. There is an important analogy between the laws of progress in the mental and the spiritual worlds. Both find their earlier sources of strength in the imaginative faculty. Intellectually we commence in the nursery with the dear old picture books, in which the giraffe, the windmill and the railway engine vie with one

----

1

British politician; 1st Viscount Morley of Blackburn

another for our affection and respect. From this we pass to a higher period of mental discipline when we learn uninteresting arithmetical tables and struggle with pot-hooks[2]. Later we arrive at the assimilation of truth in the abstract, from which lofty eminence we look down with some amusement and contempt upon our earlier weakness.

It is not otherwise in that higher intellectual region which Dr. Jowett terms the "realm of the spirit." The deepest truths come to men most readily in a pictorial form. The imagination can grasp with certainty what the undisciplined mind cannot, from sheer inexpertness, lay hold of at all. Thus, when a professor from the colleges discourses to an average congregation upon theological truth in the abstract, they esteem him dry and unintelligible. It is like teaching trigonometry and the differential calculus to the infant class. Dr. Jowett meets their case by combining something of the subtlety of the theologian with the simplest and most elemental forms of expression. He carries his hearers back to the picture book and nursery stage of their spiritual experience. He contrives to teach them much the same lesson as his more academic friend, but he accomplishes it by interesting them in the pictures and leaving them to imbibe the truth which they represent.

If there is one thing in which he may be said to be carrying on the work of his old teacher at Edinburgh, Professor Henry Drummond, it is in the direction of what Drummond himself used to describe as "spiritual diagnosis."

The preachers of the day may be divided roughly into three classes, represented by three well-known and easily distinguished types. There is the dogmatic theologian, engaged in the frontal attack on unfaith in its intellectual capacity; there is the religious politician, conducting a kind of guerilla warfare against the social enemy; and there is the spiritual physician

---

2   A curved stroke in handwriting, esp. as made by children learning to write

who follows with the main body, and undertakes the much needed task of tending the wounded for the other two. It is to this last class that Dr. Jowett unquestionably belongs. If I may be pardoned a somewhat daring but not inappropriate metaphor, I would say that he is the Florence Nightingale of the Nonconformist Church militant. He feels but little drawn to the long-range artillery with which a scientific theology seeks to reduce the citadel of a rampant unbelief. He is far too sensitive and highly strung to engage in the rough and tumble of the political skirmish. But he loves to wander among the defeated and disabled in Christ's army, cheering with a word here, consoling with a promise there, now bringing word of a new victory at a particular point, now inspiring enthusiasm and hope by confident prediction of ultimate triumph.

Dr. Jowett brings to the task many of the qualifications of the physician. To begin with, he is an incurable optimist. The note of pessimism is incompatible with his outlook on life, still less with the gospel which he preaches. Even if the nature of his subject occasionally leads him to dwell upon the sombre reality of facts, it is only that he may brandish aloft amid the darkness which he has created the glowing torch of hope. He contrives to see bright edges to the darkest and most forbidding clouds. His recently published little book, entitled The Silver Lining, is a study in eclipses—a "First Aid to the Spiritually Wounded," an "Enquire Within" upon everything concerning the disaffections of the soul.

But Dr. Jowett is not merely an optimist; he accomplishes the further task of interesting men in the remedy he is proposing to apply, and thus calls in their volitionary powers as conscious helpers in their own recovery. I remember hearing of a man who, throughout a serious illness, evinced such a scientific interest in his symptoms that his medical man permitted him to record his own temperature three times a day, and keep a record of the same extending over a period of three weeks. His recovery was not a little due to the healthy stimulus of mental interest. Dr. Jowett does something analogous to this in the spiritual realm. In other words he makes a practice of preaching the elementary psychology of the heart, in order that his hearers may understand something of the mysterious laws by which their moral recovery is to be brought about. It is in these periods of analysis that Dr. Jowett rises to the fulness of his powers. He is never quite so interesting and convincing as when he deliberately commits himself to a piece of lucid and consistent reasoning.

Probably Dr. Jowett himself hardly realizes the extent to which he relies upon his ability to create an artificial atmosphere congenial to his peculiar mode of thought. This he accomplishes almost unconsciously, though he frequently assists it by a preliminary challenge to the imagination of his audience. For this he is indebted to that brilliant flow of imagery of which his mind seems to be a perfectly inexhaustible reservoir. Take as an example the following description of an Arab fleeing to a desert tent:

"This is a desert scene. A hot, panting fugitive is fleeing for his life, pursued and hunted by the forces of a fierce revenge. His crime is placarded on his garments; the marks of blood are upon him. In a moment of passion, or in cool deliberateness, he has maimed and outraged his brother. And now fear has spurred him to flight. Nemesis is upon his track. He takes to the desert! The wild, inhospitable waste stretches before him in shadowless immensity. No bush offers him a secret shelter; no rock offers him a safe defence. He can almost feel the hot breath of his pursuers in the rear. Whither shall he turn? His terrified eyes search the horizon, and in the cloudy distance he discerns the dim outlines of a desert-tent. His excited nerves play like whips about his muscles, and with terrific strain he makes for the promised rest. The way is long! The enemy is near! The air is feverish! The night is falling! The runner is faint! Spurring himself anew and flinging all his wasting resources into the flight with the pursuers even at his

heels, he stretches out towards the mark, and with one last tremendous exertion he touches the tent rope and is safe. He is now the guest of the desert man, and the guest is inviolable. All the hallowed sanctions of hospitality gather about him in his defence. He is taken into the tent, food is placed before him, while his evaded pursuers stand frowningly at the door. The fugitive is at rest! Such is the undimmed glory of Arab hospitality. (from the *The Silver Lining*)"

Considered as part of a spoken utterance, this passage is a masterpiece of vivid and graphic description. The short, terse sentences, the almost complete absence of apparent effort, the condensation, yet withal the trembling vitality of the passage, reveal the true art of narration and make you suffer in sympathy with the pursued. This passage, coming as it does at the very commencement of a sermon, accomplishes the two-fold object of introducing the subject and establishing vital contact between the speaker's rapidly moving thought and the imaginations of his hearers. From that moment he has his audience in his grip. The rest is merely a question of sustained interest.

The opening paragraph of "Light all the Way" is a good example of Dr. Jowett's power of word painting, with its wonderful suggestion of tranquility—the quiet softness of breaking dawn merging into the heightening splendours of the sunrise seen from some lonely and commanding height.

An interesting example of how Dr. Jowett will sometimes take a central thought and present it again and again, as it were, under varying angles of illumination, the little discourse entitled "Our Brilliant Moments" from "The Silver Lining" might be suitably chosen. The preacher has been wandering recently along a winding hilly road on a dark and stormy night. An intense darkness hides the distance from his view, and even the nearest objects loom weirdly out of the obscurity. Suddenly the clouds part, the moon sweeps into the rift, and in a flood of light the road stands out like a white ribbon across the hill and the whole countryside emerges into view. The rift closes. The darkness again reigns supreme. But the traveller has taken his bearings and can proceed with assured tread. From this simple illustration he proceeds to enunciate the principle of believing in the moment of inspiration. "While ye have light, believe in the light,: and the idea is successfully worked out in its individual and national relationships.

Dr. Jowett's prayers are perhaps, the most beautiful of all his public utterances. Here he abandons all the artifices of gesture and expression which mark his sermons and speaks with the simplicity which becomes the approach of human weakness into the Eternal Presence. When you have once heard this grey-haired young man, humbly yet with conscious dignity, supplicating on behalf of erring men before the invisible throne of grace, you have gained a new vision of the poetry of English speech and a new consciousness of the majesty of things unseen.

Extract from *J. H. Jowett - A Character Study*, Chapter V. *Some Impressions – Frank Morison, 1911.*

CHAPTER ONE

The School of Calvary

"For to me to live is Christ"— Philippians 1:21

THERE are three cardinal words in the passage: "me," "live," "Christ." The middle term "live" is defined in the union of the two extremes. The two carbon electrodes of the arc lamp are brought into relationship, and the result is a light of brilliant intensity. And these two terms, "me" and "Christ," are brought into relationship, and there is revealed "the light of life," and I become "alive unto God." The human finds life in union with the divine.

Now this is the only contact which justifies the usage of the term "life." Any other application of the word is illegitimate and degrading. The word "life" stands defined in the relationship of the apostle's words. But we take other extremes, and combine them, and we name the resultant, "life."

"For me to live is money." Me — money! And we describe the union as "life." We are using a gloriously spacious and wealthy term to label a petty and superficial gratification, which is as transient and uncertain as the ephemera that dance through the feverish hour of a single summer's day.

"For me to live is pleasure!" Me — pleasure! And we describe the union as "life." It is a mere sensation, having no more relationship to life in its reality than the sluggish and ill-defined existence of the amoeba has to the large mental and spiritual exercises of the Apostle John. "She that liveth in pleasure is dead while she liveth."

"For me to live is fame" Me — fame! And we describe the union as "life." It is a mere galvanized spasm, and is no more worthy of the regal term "life" than a will-o-the-wisp is worthy of bearing the name of the sun.

Of all these relationships we may employ the New Testament indictment and say, "Thou hast a name to *live* and art dead." All other combinations fail. By no other fellowships can we produce the resultant. Life is the unique product of a unique union. "This is life, to know Jesus." "For me *to live* is Christ." Such was the rich and ineffable life of the Apostle Paul. Let us turn our thoughts upon it in prayerful meditation.

The first condition of real life is something to *love*, and the second condition is something to *revere*. For a living issue each of the elements is essential. Each deprived of the other is robbed of its dynamic.

Neither can lift if the other be absent. Love without reverence becomes a purely carnal sentiment, and resides in the channels of the flesh. Reverence without love is like cold moonlight, and will never enrich the heart with the presence of gracious flowers. Love without reverence is a destructive fever; reverence without love is a perpetual frost. True love kneels in reverence; true reverence yearns in love. Each, I say, is essential to the other, and both are needful in the creation of worthy and wealthy life.

Now, where can love and reverence be best begotten? Where can we find the atmosphere most fitted for their creation? Where can we learn to love and revere in such a way that they shall become the spontaneous exercises of the soul?

I. The School of Calvary

I sometimes take down from my bookshelves a little book of devotion written by a great mystic 300 years ago. I turn to Chapter 10 of this book and read its quaint and engaging title: "Calvary is the true academy of love." If I want a school where love is taught and revealed, I must seek the academy of Calvary! The teaching is superlatively impressive, and even the dullest scholar makes progress in the school. Let me quote from my much-sought-after devotional guide:

"The death and passion of our Lord is the gentlest, and at the same time the strongest motive which can animate our hearts in this mortal life; and it is quite true that the mystical bees make their most excellent honey in the wounds of the lion of the tribe of Judah, who was killed, shattered, and rent on Mount Calvary."

It is a quaint and very suggestive figure. Out of death, which destroys all things, "has come forth the meat" of our consolation; out of death, which is stronger than all things, "has come forth the sweetness" of the honey of our love. We are to be like bees, and we are to "make our excellent honey" in the wounds of the lion of the tribe of Judah.

Or, to return to my writer's title figure, we are to go into the academy of Calvary, which is the all-excelling school of love. And what are we to do when we get there? We are to employ the ministry of meditation.

I care not how unpractical the counsel may seem in this busy, hurrying, breathless day. If we men and women are ever to attain unto life and make progress in its ways, we have got to find time to go to school and learn.

I think one of the can't phrases of our day is the familiar one by which we express our permanent want of time. We repeat it so often that by the very repetition we have deceived ourselves into believing it. It is never the supremely busy men who have got no time. So compact and systematic is the regulation of their day, that, whenever you make a demand upon

17

them, they seem to be able to find additional corners to offer for unselfish service. I find that when I have comparatively little to pack into my portmanteau it seems as full as when I have much. The less we have to pack the more carelessly we pack it, and the portmanteau appears to be full.

There is many a man who says he has no time, who proclaims his day to be full, but the fullness is the result of careless packing. I confess, as a minister, that the men to whom I most hopefully look for additional service are the busiest men. They are always willing to squeeze another item into their bulging portmanteau.

But, even though our plea were legitimate, if our time were crowded, if the portmanteau were packed, if we cannot find a corner of the day for meditation in the school of Christ, then we must take something out and make room for it. I think if we search our bags we shall find many and many a rag which takes up space, but which is of very little worth, and which might very safely be banished.

But if even all the contents were valuables, even assuming that they were pearls, the Master has declared that the secret of progressive living is to sacrifice the pearl of inferior value for the pearl of transcendent worth. Even assuming that the newspaper is not a rag, but a jewel, I do not think it wise to cram so many into the bag that there is no room for the Book of Revelation, the title deeds of "the house not made with hands, eternal in the heavens."

No, if we mean truly to "live," we have got to find time for the highest of all exercises, meditation upon the eternal things of God. We have to go to Calvary, the academy of love, and reverently contemplate the unveilings of redemptive grace. How many of the men in our congregations ever open their Bibles for private meditation from Monday morning to Saturday night? We give ourselves no opportunity. Love and reverence are not the uncertain products of chance. They are the sure and stately products of thought. If our thought be steadily directed, love and reverence will follow in its train.

Let us go, then, into the school of Calvary, with eyes and ears alert and quickened, that we may see and hear. We shall get into the secret places of the Most High, and we shall behold the marvelous unveiling of Infinite Love. We shall hear that wondrous evangel that Pascal heard, and which melted his heart, and hallowed all his years: "I love thee more ardently than thou hast loved thy sin."

I cannot describe the tremendous impact which that sentence makes upon my life. I know how I have sinned. I know how I have clung to my sin. I know how I have yearned after it. I know what illicit pleasure I have found in it. I know how I have pursued it at any cost. And, now, in the school of Calvary, my Master takes up this, my so strenuous and overwhelming passion for sin, and contrasts it disparagingly with His passion for me: "*I love thee more than thou has loved thy sin.*" If in some quiet moment that grand evangel swept through our souls in heavenly strains, we should fall in love with the Lover, and our love would imply our entrance into eternal life.

And as for reverence — no man can go softly and thoughtfully into the school of Calvary without falling upon his knees. He is awed by what he sees, as well as by what he hears. "They gave Him vinegar to drink mingled with gall, and when He had tasted thereof, He would not drink." "And they that passed by reviled Him, wagging their heads." "Father, forgive them, they know not what they do." "Now, from the sixth hour there was darkness over the land, until the ninth hour." "My God, My God, why hast Thou forsaken Me?" "And when He had cried again with a loud voice, He yielded up the ghost." I say, go into that school — quietly, privately, and you will soon be on your knees!

The old mystic is right — Calvary is *the* academy in which we may learn reverence and love. We are wooed by the vision into surrender and spiritual fellowship, and through the gracious ministries of purification and illumination we pass into perfected union with the Lord. Love and reverence for the Highest are the conditions of true life, and in love and reverence for the Lord we attain unto eternal life, and become partakers of the divine nature. "I live, yet not I, Christ liveth in me." "For to me to *live* is Christ."

Now, let no one suppose that this mystical union with Christ drives men into fruitless reveries and idle dreams. There is no one so practical, no one so splendidly energetic, as the advanced mystic. Why, even Dr. Johnson, who I think cannot be accused of effeminacy, or of any inclination toward a weak and watery sentiment, describes the mystical saints as characterized by "vigour and efficacy." And, in truth, any one who knows the history of the saints knows that these are their pronounced public characteristics. They are vigorous; there is an optimistic robustness about their carriage. They are efficacious; their energy is directed to definite and practical ends.

The Apostle Paul was a mystic. Read the middle chapters of the Epistle to the Romans, the whole of the Epistle to the Ephesians, and all the Epistle to the Colossians, and you will learn how profound and mystical was his union with the Lord.

And was he practical? Was his life characterized by "vigour and efficacy"? Go straight from the fine, subtle, mystical thinking of the Epistle to the Romans to the busy, tumultuous doings of the Acts of the Apostles, and you will get your reply.

John Tauler was a great mystic, one of the greatest of the mystics, living in profound union with the Lord. Was he practical? Or was he a dreamer? Listen to this little extract from one of his writings: "If a man while devoutly engaged in prayer were called by some duty in the Providence of God to cease therefrom and cook a broth for some sick person, or any other such service, he should do so willingly and with great joy."

There is a practical flavour about this man's mysticism. When the Black Death raged in Strasburg John Tauler disregarded the Interdict, and worked day and night among the plague-stricken people. Surely there is something vigorous and efficacious about this man's fellowship with his Lord!

John Wesley was a mystic, led by the mystics into union with the risen Lord. For him to live was Christ! Did John Wesley pass his years in coloured reveries and dreams? Take the four volumes of his journal into your hands and find the answer. John Wesley was the greatest English figure of the eighteenth century. We cannot survey the practical life of the century without meeting him at every turn.

General Gordon was a mystic. His soldiers knew the meaning of the white handkerchief when it floated outside his tent, and the sacred privacy was not disturbed. Was he practical? The slums knew the sound of his feet, and the little waifs and strays found hospitality in the sunny rooms of his grace-blessed soul.

In all these examples the mystical union with the Lord resulted in marvelously practical energy, which issued in multiplied services for the race. "For to me to live is Christ." "He that believeth on Me, out of him shall flow rivers of living water."

When "to live is Christ" everything is claimed for Him. Everything is sealed with the King's seal, and used for His exclusive glory. Said the saintly Bengel, *"Quicquid vivo Christum vivo."* Whatever I live, I live Christ! Through whatever I am to live, I live Christ; I set upon everything the imprint of my Lord! Nothing is allowed to become an alien minister. No circumstance is allowed to raise the flag of revolt. Bengel made every circumstance in his life pay tribute to Christ.

Let me quote a little extract from an exquisite little book of Thomas Boston, a Scotch mystic, whose life was abounding in labours: "Learn that heavenly chemistry of extracting some spiritual thing out of earthly things. To this end endeavour after a heavenly frame, which will, as is recorded of the philosopher's stone, turn every metal into gold. When the soul is heavenly, it will even scrape jewels out of a dunghill."

All of this just means that a man in Christ can make his adverse environment ideal. He can make his disappointments his ministers. He can make his adversities the King's witnesses. He can make his very bereavements glorify his Lord. Whatever he lives, he lives Christ! If he lives through a season of sorrow, he lives Christ. If he lives through a season of commercial ruin, he lives Christ. If his path take him past a grave, he lives Christ! For him to live is Christ.

CHAPTER TWO

Lose to find

"He that findeth his life shall lose it; and he that loseth
his life for my sake shall find it"— Matthew 10:39

This is surely a very extraordinary chapter. As its contents
pass before us we are possessed by feelings of ever-heighten-
ing surprise. Here is Jesus, gathering about Him a little company of twelve men. No member of the little band belongs to the
ranks of power, or culture, or wealth. They are all inconspicu-
ous, many of them unlettered, the majority of them poor; it is
just a company of working men standing nervously on the bor-
ders of an unfamiliar publicity.

And now their Master is about to send them forth to proclaim and perpetuate His ministry. With what kind of program
will He inspire them? What glory of possibility will He set before them? What light will He place upon the distant horizon
to cheer them in their mission? What will He say to kindle in
the hearts of these timid toilers a burning and insatiable enthusiasm?

When I turn to the program, I wonder at the oppressive-
ness of the shadow. I wonder that the Master uses such black
colours in depicting the coming day. "Ye shall be brought before governors and kings for My sake." "Ye shall be hated of

all men for My name's sake." "When they persecute you in one city, flee ye into another." "A man's foes shall be they of his own household." "He that taketh not his cross, and followeth after Me, is not worthy of Me."

I am amazed at the almost audacious candour of the program. There is no hiding of the sharp flint, no softening of the shadow, no gilding of the cross. The hostilities bristle in naked obtrusiveness. Every garden is a prospective battlefield "I am not come to send peace, but a sword." The choice of the Christ involves a perpetual challenge to war.

Now, if this be the program of the kingdom, what shall we do? What are we tempted to do? We are tempted to frame for ourselves a very perverted conception of the characteristics of a reasonable life. If our surrounding can be so hostile, if our difficulties can be so stupendous, if the hatred we may awake can be so intense, if we can call into being a mighty army of aliens, surely the policy dictated by a sane and healthy judgment will be this: Take the line of least resistance; keep your lips closed; go with the stream; look after yourself!

This is the method of reasonableness! This is the policy which assures self-preservation! This is the secret of a successful and progressive life! Keep your lips closed — the policy of silence; go with the stream — the policy of opportunism; look after yourself — the policy of self-aggrandizement. Such is the counsel of Mr. Worldly Wiseman, who strenuously urges upon me this threefold policy of silence, drifting, and suction, if amid all these sleeping hostilities I would attain to a roomy and successful life.

Now, in the chapter before us the Master absolutely reverses the counsel. Not by the policy of the world shall we ever attain to self-preservation and enrichment; it is a policy which speedily and inevitably leads to impoverishment and self-destruction. The policy of the world leads to an apparent "finding'" in reality it is a terrible "losing." Along these roads the apparent finder is the loser; the apparent loser is the winner.

Let us proclaim the methods of the Lord. It is not by silence, but by expression that we win; "Whoever shall confess Me before men." It is not by drifting, but by endurance that we win; "He that endureth to the end shall be saved." It is not be self-aggrandizement but by self-sacrifice that we win; "He that loseth his life for My sake shall find it." This is the secret of Jesus; life is sustained and enriched by expression, by endurance, and by sacrifice.

Let us now apply these principles of the Master to the individual life. Take the first — life is secured and enriched by expression. Apply the policy of silence to the domain of the feelings. Feelings which are never expressed languish away and die. It is equally true of the noble and the base. Refuse expression to an unworthy passion and we slay it by suffocation. Love that never tells its story, that never utters itself in word, or gift, or service, fades away into drowsy indifference. Sympathy that never becomes incarnate congeals into cold benumbment. Gratitude that never testifies soon ceases to be felt.

Pursue the policy of silence in the matter of the sentiments, and we shall speedily be despoiled of our wealth. Our feelings require an outlet; they are oxygenated in speech. The price of retention is expression. We must give them out if we would keep them in. We must lose them if we would find them.

Apply the policy of silence to the acquisition of a truth. A truth that is never proclaimed is never really known. Truth reserves her rarest beauties for the moment when she is being shared. If we retain her we only see her partially; if we give her away we see her "in new lights." In the moment of communication she reveals an unsuspected wealth. The teacher gains more knowledge while he is giving away what he knows.

Truth is vivified in the very ministry of expression. "What I tell you in the ear, that proclaim ye upon the house tops!"

Perhaps our Master intended to suggest that we never see the full glory of truth when we receive it; the full glory will break upon us only when we proclaim it. Never tell the truth, and the truth will always remain dim; proclaim it, and it will emerge from the mist in clear and most alluring outline. The price of retention is expression. We must lose if we would find.

Take the second of the principles given us by our Lord — the purposes of life are not served by the policy of drifting, but by the ministry of resistance. Life is energized by endurance. Drifting may be the secret of easy living; it never discovers the entrance into a spacious life. To go with the stream may be a luxury, but it is a luxuriousness which is productive of a perilous enervation. We can never drift into any really worthy and permanent wealth.

We can never drift into rest. The only people who never find rest are the idle and the indolent. The preparative to rest is labour, and rest only reveals its rich and essential flavours to those who have plodded the ways of toil. It is the men who have lost who find. Rest never visits the idle man, even though he have an easy chair in every room in the house. "Strive to enter into rest."

We can never drift into joy. The only people who are strangers to joy are the people who shirk every difficulty, and never contend with a troublesome task. It requires a little pressure even to get the juice out of a grape, and it does seem as though the fine juices of life are only tasted where there is a certain stress and strain, a certain pressure, a certain sense of burden and task. The precious juice of joy is never the perquisite of the drifter; it visits the lips of resistance and is the fruit of conquest. "Enter thou into the joy of thy Lord"; that is the commanding issue of prolonged strife and resistance.

We never drift into strength. Drifting makes no muscle; the muscle is impoverished. The man who drifts with the stream appears to be conserving his strength, while in reality the ease is just the measure of the leakage. It is the man who appears to be expending strength who is really gaining it; the man toiling at the oar and resisting the stream, he acquires the power of the stream he resists. The policy of drifting appears to find, but it loses; the policy of resistance and endurance appears to lose, but it grandly finds. "He that findeth his life shall lose it; and he that loseth his life for My sake shall find it."

Take the third of the principles proclaimed by the Lord — it is not by the policy of self-aggrandizement that we can find the secrets of an enduring progress. Life is not enriched by selfishness, but by sacrifice. Life becomes fruitful only when it becomes sacrificial. This is true concerning our influence upon one another. It seems ordained that life has to attain a certain fervour of sacrifice before it can become contagious and multiply itself throughout the race. On the cold planes of calculation and selfishness life is unimpressive, and its products leave the general life unmoved.

It is even so with a poem, with a painting, with a sermon, ay! With a courtesy; the measure of its impressiveness is just the measure of the sacrifice of which it is the shrine. What is there in the poem of the heart, of energy, of blood? What has the man put into it? What did he lose in its making? What "virtue" has gone out of him? Just so much will be the measure of healing. Just what he lost will be our gain; he becomes fruitful where he touches sacrifice.

But let us say more — the poet himself is the gainer by so much as he lost. The spirit of sacrifice not only impresses others, it fertilizes self. In the fervent atmosphere of sacrifice buried seeds of possibility awake into life, which in an air of cold calculation remain in their graves — powers of perception, of resolution, of effort. In the tropical heat of sacrifice they spring into strength and beauty.

I say, therefore, that the spirit of sacrifice enriches self while yet it fertilizes others. Our giving is our getting. "With what measure ye mete, it shall be measured to you again."

Here, then, are the gates to a rich and roomy individual life; not silence, but expression; not drifting, but endurance; not self-seeking, but sacrifice; for "he that findeth his life shall lose it, but he that loseth his life for My sake shall find it."

Now let me lift up the principles to a larger application. I have tried to reveal their relationship to the individual, but they are equally applicable to wider relationships — to families, to societies, to states, and to the Church.

Let me confine this larger outlook to the life of the Church. Here is the Church of Christ placed in an environment of sleeping hostilities. If she moves, her foes awake and arrange themselves in serried ranks. Here and there she meets with violent hatred, and everywhere she is confronted with gigantic tasks. The difficulties are here in our homeland, and they are multiplied in lands afar.

What shall be our policy? We may not definitely formulate the policy, and by the very absence of a clear and strong decision we may be snared into the three perilous worldly policies of silence, drifting, and self-aggrandizement; a policy of silence, not proclaiming in every place the evangel which we have received; a policy of drifting, evading the enormous tasks and difficulties of the almost immeasurable field of service; a policy of self-aggrandizement, appropriating the ministries of grace to our own consolation, and sitting and singing ourselves "away to everlasting bliss."

And here, again, is the word of the Saviour. By the methods of the world the Church will never gain her life. Life gained in such conditions is miserably delusive. The vitality is only apparent. The growth is dropsical. The finding is only a losing. The Church that would grow rich must externalize and invest its treasure. The Church that would live must die. If she would have her Olivet of enriched communion, she must seek it by the way of Golgotha and the Cross. If she would gain, she must lose. She must be a missionary Church, working out her salvation by the ministries of expression, endurance, and sacrifice.

How would she gain? Turn again to our principles. The life of the Church is secured and enriched by expression. I do not think the Church ever discovers the manifold wealth of her evangel until she begins to proclaim it to the varied and manifold needs of the race. Its adaptability to diverse circumstances brings strange corroboration to its truth.

It is even so on the plane of matter. On the material plane a scientific discoverer hungers for a multiplicity of tests. He longs to give his theory the trial of multiplied experiments. The larger and more varied the range, the more illumined and assured becomes his conviction. And here is the evangel of the Christ. We can only apprehend it partially if we confine its application to our own needs. Set it in a different light, and it will reveal an unsuspected glory.

Take it to India; bring it to bear upon the Hindoo; set it side by side with his sad and dreary religion; let the Father of the Lord Jesus Christ be seen in contrast with his own deity, inaccessible to human affection, or, indeed, to anything else; proclaim the duty and privilege of holiness amid conditions which give little emphasis to morals. Do all this, and it requires but little imagination to see that our evangel will assume an undiscovered majesty and glory, which will warm and illumine the minds and hearts of its own heralds.

Take it among the primitive islanders of the South Pacific; take it among the keen and sinewy natives of Central Africa; take it among the half-awake and conservative people of China; take it among the alert, absorbent, and prospecting Japanese; and every new application will reveal a new adaptability of "the exceeding richness of His grace."

We discover while we evangelize. Our torch emits new flame while we light the lamps of others. We get while we give. "He that findeth his life shall lose it; he that loseth his life for My sake shall find it."

Again, the principle is true in wider relationships. The life of the Church is energized and enriched by endurance. The difficulties of home and foreign missionary work are gigantic. No field has been discovered where the difficulty is absent. The line of least resistance is to remain at ease. But the path to ease is not the way to life. A difficulty should always be interpreted as an invitation. If the Church be healthy, a great task will always be an allurement. For difficulties are only rightly interpreted when they are regarded as promises.

Every difficulty contains prospective wealth. Break it open, and the wealth is yours! We appropriate the strength of the enemy we vanquish. Overcome a difficulty, and its power henceforth enlists on our side. That is a grand evangel, having application both to individual and to common life.

There are monster difficulties in China. Let the Christian Church overcome them, and the force of the monster difficulties is added to her strength. We are energized by our tasks. Our muscle is made by our resistances. And, therefore, you will find that the seasons of commanding difficulty have ever been the seasons of the Church's exuberant health. The strong negative has begotten mighty affirmative. The forces of persecution have produced sterling muscle and inflexible resolve.

Let us, therefore, look at difficulties as promises in the guise of tasks. They are treasure houses presenting the appearance of bristling forts. Break them open, I say, and the treasure is yours. To dare is to win! "He that loseth his life shall find it."

And as for the third principle, only a word need be said. The life of the Church becomes fruitful when it becomes sacrificial. When the church is easeful she loses the power to redeem. I remember the old story of Pope Innocent IV and Thomas Aquinas, who were standing together as bags of treasure were being carried in through the gates of the Lateran.

"You see," observed the Pope, with a smile, "the day is past when the Church could say, 'Silver and gold have I none!'"

"Yes, Holy Father," was the saint's reply, "and the day is past when the Church could say to the lame man, 'Rise and walk!'"

When the church's life is lived on the plane of ease, and comfort, and bloodless service, she has no power to fertilize the dry and barren places of the earth. When the Church becomes sacrificial, she becomes impressive. The sacrificial things in history are the influential things today.

It is the men and the women who give away their being, the bleeding folk, who are our present inheritance. The woman who gave the two mites still works as a factor in the life of the race. Sir John Kelynge — have you ever heard of him? — the brutal, cynical justice who thrust John Bunyan for twelve years into Bedford gaol, his very name is now a conundrum! John Bunyan, the sacrificial martyr, is still fertilizing the field of common life with energies of rich inspiration.

The finders have lost. The apparent losers are at the winning post! The sacrificial are the triumphant. "They loved not their lives unto the death, and they overcame by the blood of the Lamb." A sacrificial Church would speedily conquer the world! "He that findeth his life shall lose it; and he that loseth his life for My sake shall find it."

CHAPTER THREE

The Sufferings of Christ

*"For as the sufferings of Christ abound unto us, even
so our comfort also aboundeth through Christ"*
— 2 Corinthians 1:5

And that word "sufferings," when used by the Apostle
Paul, is not a big term to express a very little thing. "For we
would not have you ignorant, brethren, concerning our affliction which befell us in Asia, that we were weighed down ex-
ceedingly, beyond our power, insomuch that we despaired even
of life."

And still later in the same letter we have another glimpse
of the apostle in suffering. "In stripes above measure, in pris-
ons more frequent, in death oft, of the Jews five times received
I forty stripes save one. Thrice was I beaten with rods, once I
was stoned, thrice I suffered shipwreck, a night and a day I
have been in the deep; in journeyings often, in perils of waters,
in perils of robbers, in perils by mine own countrymen, in per-
ils by the heathen, in perils in the city, in perils in the wilderness, in perils in the sea, in perils among false brethren, in
weariness and painfulness, in watchings often, in hunger and
thirst, in fastings often, in cold and nakedness."

And yet, in the very midst of this tumultuous narrative, like bird song in a thunderstorm, there rises this melodious assurance — "As the sufferings of Christ abound unto us, even so our comfort also aboundeth through Christ."

It is a strange conjunction this of "suffering" and "comfort." And it is all the more strange when they are put together in the relation of cause and effect, and comfort emerges from suffering as springs have been loosened by the earthquake at Messina, as volcanic influences are productive of conditions which feed the most luxurious vines.

But apostolic teaching is also the teaching of common experience. Apart altogether from the Christian revelation, men have learned that affliction and consolation, suffering and blessedness, are not alien and mutually repellent, but related by affinities vital and profound.

Even Positivism, which is just a vast scheme of benevolence comprehending every form of sentient life, and which aims at universal blessedness, "decks itself out in the blood-stained garment of Christian asceticism," and in order to gain happiness employs the ministry of sacrifice. One of the primary precepts or principles of Positivism is just this — either suffer or die!

But the teaching which links the volcano and the vine, the earthquake and the springs, suffering and blessedness, affliction and emancipation, is preeminently significant of the Christian religion. It found its symbol of life in the minister of apparent death. Its emblem of victory is a cross, and its ascending transitions are crucifixions. It fashions its glories out of seeming shame, as the loveliest hues are extracted from the blackest pitch.

It has only one path into life — a strait gate and a narrow way; it has only one secret of joyful liberty — self-sacrifice and vigilant self-restraint. "If any man will be My disciple, let him deny himself, and take up his cross and follow Me." We can obtain the wine of life only through the crushing of the grapes. Affliction introduces us to the juices and the mannas. "For as the sufferings of Christ abound unto us, even so our comfort also aboundeth through Christ."

And so let us turn our minds in quiet meditation upon those "sufferings of Christ" in which fellowship we are to find our consolation. And let us, first of all, remind ourselves of the words in which our Lord described His holy purpose and ministry: "He hath anointed Me to preach the gospel to the poor; He hath sent Me to heal the brokenhearted, to preach deliverance to the captives, and recovering of sight to the blind, to set at liberty them that are bruised." Such is the range and richness of our Lord's redemptive mission.

Now, the range of our possible sufferings is determined by the largeness and nobility of our aims. It is possible to evade a multitude of sorrows by the cultivation of an insignificant life. Indeed, if it be a man's ambition to avoid the troubles of life, the recipe is perfectly simple — let him shed his ambitions in every direction, let him cut the wings of every soaring purpose, and let him assiduously cultivate a little life, with the fewest correspondences and relations.

By this means a whole continent of afflictions will be escaped and will remain unknown. Cultivate negations, and large tracts of the universe will cease to exist. For instance, cultivate deafness, and you are saved from the horrors of discords. Cultivate blindness, and you are saved from the assault of the ugly. Stupefy a sense, and you shut out a world. And, therefore, it is literally true that if you want to get through the world with the smallest trouble you must reduce yourself to the smallest compass.

And, indeed, that is why so many people, and even so many professedly Christian people get through life so easily, and with a minimum acquaintance with tribulation. It is because they have reduced their souls to a minimum, that their course through the years is not so much the transit of a man as the passage of an amoeba.

They have no finely organized nervous system, or they have deadened and arrested the growth of one nerve after another; they have cut the sensitive wires which bind the individual to the race, and they are cosily self-contained, and the shuddering sorrow of the world never disturbs their seclusion. Tiny souls can dodge through life; bigger souls are blocked on every side.

As soon, therefore, as a man begins to enlarge his life, his resistances are multiplied. Let a man tear out of his soul the petty selfish purpose and enthrone a world purpose, the Christ purpose, and his sufferings will be increased on every side. Every addition to spiritual ambition widens the exposure of the soul, and sharpens its perception of the world's infirmity and the sense of its own restraints. How then was it with that vast spiritual ambition of the Saviour which He Himself described in words which I have quoted from the Gospel by Luke? That all-absorbing redemptive purpose was bound to introduce Him to ceaseless suffering.

First of all, there were the sufferings which were incident to the very existence of a majestic purpose. Vast ambitions are not kept burning in the soul without fuel. They suck the very energies of the body into their own flame. Fine passion makes a heavy drain upon the nerves; the suburbs are scoured to feed the fire at the centre. There is not a man or woman of holy Christian passion today who is not "burning the candle at both ends." They cannot help it.

And the consequence is they experience the sufferings which are incident to the limitations of the flesh. The body is too frail for the fiery spirit. The steed is exhausted while the driver is quite fresh. And, therefore, do these passionate hearts suffer in the imprisonment of their own physical restraints. "I have a baptism to be baptized with, and how am I straitened!"

And do you wonder, as you read the record of the sacred life, that you come upon significant words like these: "And Jesus, being wearied, sat thus by the well." "And He was in the hinder part of the ship, asleep on a pillow." May I say it reverently — it was the tired-out body, the exhausted minister which carried the holy, passionate redemptive purpose of God.

And, second, there were His sufferings which were incident to the passive antagonism of the indifferent. I mention these before I mention the antagonism of His positive foes because I think they inflict a deeper wound. The fiery crusader can meet an active opponent and overthrow him, but what can he do with the indifferent who have not a spark of concern? If you are passionate about anything, the indifference of others will make you wonder; if it is a moral enthusiasm, the indifference will give you pain. "Is it nothing to you, all ye that pass by?"

That is the cry of a wounded spirit. They would not even turn aside to glance at the pearl of great price! I think there is no crucifixion for the spiritually chivalrous man equal to that which is inflicted by the unconcern of those whom he seeks to redeem.

There is on sentence in James Gilmour's diary which was surely written in blood. It was written after years of labour. "In the shape of converts I have seen no result. I have not, as far as I am aware, seen any one who even *wanted* to be a Christian."

And that was the experience of a man who, when he arrived at his field of labour, had written these words in his diary: "Several huts in sight! When shall I be able to speak to the people? O Lord, suggest by the Spirit how I should come among them, and guide me in gaining the language, and in preparing myself to teach the life and love of Christ Jesus!...I have not, as far as I am aware, seen any one who even wanted to be a Christian." Surely that was "the fellowship of His sufferings!"

And third, there were His sufferings which were incident to the active antagonism of His foes. There are the sufferings occasioned by passivity, but there are also the sufferings occasioned by hostility. One man has no interest in your message; the other listens and rejects. One man scarcely lifts his eyes to look at you. "So was it in the days of Noah!"

The other stands up to you and declares you have a devil. Your aims are distorted, your spirit is misinterpreted; you are said to be wearing a stolen livery, assuming a benevolent purpose while you are seeking your own ends. And so it was with our Lord and Saviour Jesus Christ. "He came unto His own, and His own received Him not." Hostilities were multiplied. "He was despised and rejected of men, a man of sorrows and acquainted with grief."

Now all these sufferings are sufferings which we can partially share with our Lord. There are other of his sufferings, mysterious and awful, of which we may know little or nothing.

> "We may not know, we cannot tell
> What pains He had to bear."

Those secrets are yet enfolded in gross darkness; and all that we at present know is this — that out of the darkness, as from black subterranean depths, there flows "a river of water of life, clear as crystal," medicinal, strong in gracious healing, and carrying the virtuous energies of moral and spiritual transformation. There is something here which we can never share. "It is finished."

But the other sufferings I named we must and we shall share, if we share the largeness of His purpose, and in our own degree seek the moral and spiritual redemption of the race. There is a space left for your energies and mine, and therefore for your sufferings and mine: we can "fill up that which is lacking of the affliction of Christ."

And now, for one moment, I turn the matter around. "For as the sufferings of Christ abound unto us, even so our comfort also aboundeth through Christ." If we have fellowship in the one, we shall have fellowship in the other. I have already said that if we lessened our lives we should lessen our sorrows. It is now needful to add that if we lessen our lives we also lessen our joys. Deaden the sense of hearing and you escape the discords, but you also lose the harmonies. Drug your artistic sense, and you lose the pain of the ugly, but you also lose the inspiration of the lovely.

If by the enlargement of my life I let in human sorrow, I also let in divine consolation. A big, holy purpose makes me more sensitive toward the sin and hostility of man, but it also makes me more sensitive toward God. If the sufferings abound, "so our comfort aboundeth also." If I said nothing more than this, this alone would suffice; if we suffer with Christ, Christ Himself becomes a great reality. When life is a picnic, we play with theology; when life becomes a campaign, we grope for a religion. It is one thing sounding when your boat is in the open see; it is another thing sounding when the menacing rocks are on every side.

When we suffer with Christ, we come to know Christ, to come face to face with reality, and the idle superfluities drop away. "And our comfort also aboundeth through Christ." Our fellowship with His sorrows makes us receptive of His joys; "My joy shall be in you, and your joy shall be full." Our fellowship in His battles makes us receptive of his peace; "My peace I give unto you."

There is no surer way of becoming sure of Christ than to follow the way of sacrificial life and service. It may bring us into a fiery furnace of suffering, but "in the midst of the fire" there shall be One "like unto the Son of God."

CHAPTER FOUR

The Neglected Cup

"The fellowship of His sufferings" — Philippians 3:10

Let us continue our meditation on "the fellowship of His sufferings." The phrase is taken from the eager speech of a veteran apostle! One would have felt its fitness and congeniality upon the lips of a young man, some fresh, enthusiastic knight, with his armour just newly belted about him, and setting out from the threshold upon some crusade of valorous enterprise. In such conditions this strenuous speech would have been congenial, and there would have been nothing startling in its proclamation — "I set out" that I may know Him, and "the fellowship of His sufferings!"

But old men speak naturally of retirement; their fighting days are over; and they leave the stern encounter to the younger men. They often speak of having earned their rest, and the blazing ambitions of their earlier days have become cool. They no longer covet the "hardness" of the battlefield; they steal through the green pastures and by the still waters in the soft light of the setting sun.

But here is an old man with all the impetuous ambitions of his prime. His burning zeal makes even the enthusiasm of young Timothy seem dim, and he contends with the foremost of the youths for the hottest parts of the field.

He is in prison now, but he is like some stabled hunter which hears the cry of the hounds. He is as tense and eager as ever. His ambitions are a young man's ambitions; his very speech is a young man's speech; his metaphors and similes are just those which leap most readily to the lips of youth; they are sought, not from sleeping boats in the harbour, or from quiet flocks in the meadows, but from the straining, strenuous worlds of the racecourse, the amphitheatre, and the gymnasium.

And so here he is, in the very van of the Lord's hosts, in the very fighting line, ambitious to share with his Lord the central hardships of the strife. "That I may know Him . . . and the fellowship of His sufferings."

"The *fellowship* of His sufferings!" That is a great New Testament word, and especially is it one of the great determining words in the speech of the Apostle Paul. Let us enter into its wealth through this little gate which I find in the Acts of the Apostles. "And they had all things *in common*." The little phrase, "in common," is closely akin to the word, "Fellowship," and by the help of the one we may gain a clear interpretation of the other. "They had all things in common"; they had a common room and a common table, and they all shared alike in the abundance or impoverishment of the feast.

And so, too, there is a table at which our Master sits, spread with the things which He and His have to eat and drink. And we, too, may have "all things in common" with Him; nay, it is the high sign and seal of discipleship that we do sit with Him at the common board.

But here is our frequent mistake, that we regard that table as laden only with welcome provisions, and even with delicate and dainty luxuries. On that table there is the provision of peace, and the provision of joy, and the provision of glory!

And over all the table, from end to end of it, there is the soft and healing light of grace. That is how we think of the table, and, blessed be God, all these rare provisions are surely to be found at the feast; and we may have all these things "in common" with the Lord.

But there is also another cup on the table, a cup that is very near the Master's hand, a cup which we very frequently forget or ignore. It is a bitter cup, the cup of the Lord's sufferings. "Are ye able to drink of the cup that I drink of?" Are we prepared to have "*all* things in common"? We drink the cup of kindness, the overflowing cup of redeeming grace. "Are ye able to drink of the cup that I drink of?"

"I have tasted," I think I hear him say, "I have tasted and seen how gracious He is. I have drunk the cup of His salvation; but I thirst for a deeper communion still; not only the sweet and palatable cup, but that dark and bitter cup would I taste; that cup whose contents are as blood. I would have 'all things in common'! 'I count all things but loss . . . that I may know Him . . . and the fellowship of His sufferings.'"

Now our intimacy with the Lord can best be estimated by our knowledge of the contents of that bitter cup. Other things upon the table have their significance, and to taste them argues a certain measure of acquaintance with the King; but the deeper significance gathers about that cup of darker hue. The quality of our fellowship with the Lord is best revealed, not by our capacity for joy, but by our capacity for suffering. We often test our communion with the Lord by the measure of our equanimity. If our life is calm and passive, and the wrinkles are absent from our brow, and we can sing, "Peace, perfect peace!" then we assume that our intimacy with the Lord must be very deep and true.

But equanimity is a virtue very much misunderstood, and its popular representative is often only a well-disguised indifference. "Peace" is often used to label undignified and worldly ease, and as such it denotes no sort of fellowship with the Lord. There is an equanimity which is death. We do not reveal our high spiritual kinship by our ability to remain unruffled, but by our capacity to be stirred. It is when life is upheaved to its depths that we know the Lord; it is when deep calleth unto deep that we have the conditions of vital communion.

And so it is not by our pleasures, but by our pangs that we may discover our likeness to the Lord. "Are ye able to drink of the cup that I drink of?" That is the cup we forget, and yet it is in the cup of suffering that we attain the finest and rarest spiritual communion.

And yet how far from this is the common reasoning! We say one to another, "Have you found peace?" — and if an affirmative answer be returned, we give glory to God; and well we may, for to have drunk the cup of spiritual peace is a sure witness that we are found at the table of the Lord.

But how far has our fellowship advanced? How rarely we ask one another, "Have you become a partaker of the sufferings of Christ? Have you lifted that cup to your lips? And if so, when and how and where did you taste the bitter draught?"

I am afraid that if we were subjected to these most searching questions the majority of us would have to confess that we had kept our eyes upon the other parts of the table, and that we had confined ourselves to the sparkling and welcome draughts of spiritual delight. But it is a shallow intimacy which confines itself to the pleasures of the table; the deeper discipleship lays hold of the darker cup, and enters into "the fellowship of His sufferings."

Now what is there in that much neglected cup? What is the bitterness which we can have in common with the Lord? What darker experiences can we share with Him? Nay, what is it we must share before we are kinsmen worthy of the name?

Well, no one can be long in the presence of the Saviour without noticing that He always drank a bitter cup when He came into the presence of sin. The prevailing sin*hurt* Him, it crucified His spirit long before it crucified His flesh. Here is Jerusalem, wicked, wayward and indifferent, wasting its hallowed treasure in decorated debauchery. And the Master gazes upon its unholy pleasures and shames, and He weeps! Have we entered into the fellowship of that suffering? Have we tasted that cup? Or have we been so fascinated by the glittering decoration as to be oblivious to the debauchery?

Let us look at the Master, Jesus Christ, again, as He lifts to His lips the bitter cup. "And Jesus stooped downs, and with His finger wrote on the ground." Can you feel what is going on there? Have you never listened to a questionable or unclean story, and, even while it was being told, for very shame you have not known where to fix your modest eyes? "And Jesus stooped down, and with His finger wrote on the ground." He was, at that very moment, drinking the bitter cup, and when we share His burning shame, we enter into "the fellowship of His sufferings."

But how few there are who share it! We are interested in sin; we can lift our eyes in delighted inquisitiveness; we can follow its unclean track down column after column of reeking print, and we never hurl the record away in weeping and consuming shame. Sin attracts us, it does not blister us; it interests, it does not burn. We can gaze upon it in curious observation, and it does not create an emotional convulsion. We can see it and laugh; we can see it and sleep.

The Master saw it and wept. What a discord is to a refined and disciplined ear, so, in immeasurably deeper degree, should sin be to the intimate companions of Christ. What a coarse daub is to a well-trained and interpreting eye, so should sin be to eyes that have been anointed with the eye salve of grace. The sin of the city should make all true Christians smart. But does it? Do we suffer with our suffering Lord? Or is that a cup whose bitter draught we have not drunk?

Have you ever marked that word in the Book of Ezra, when that sensitive soul had discovered the sin of his people? "I fell upon my knees, and spread out my hands unto the Lord my God: and I said, O my God, I am ashamed and blush to lift up my face to Thee!" The suppliant and his Lord were just then drinking out of the same cup.

But how frequently in our life the shame is missing, and the blush is absent, and there is no suffering, no pain! And, therefore, it is that because there is no pain at sin; there is no haste to remove it. We are slow footed because we are slow to burn.

Our feet will become "like hinds' feet" when there is a burning shame in our souls, and when we taste the unutterable bitterness of all sin. We shall be swift in the ways and ministeries of redemption when we have entered into "the fellowship of His sufferings."

And that cup again! What else can we share, if our Saviour and we are to have "all things in common"? We cannot be long with the Lord without noting how deeply He suffered with the sufferings of others. Other folk's sorrows He made His own, and He drank deeply of everybody's bitter cup. Have we entered into the fellowship of those sufferings? You may possibly reply, "I've got enough of my own!"

Yes, and that is perhaps the very reason why you have so many! Personal sorrows, selfishly nursed, become more burdensome by the nursing. Many times have I known a personal grief nursed into an intolerable load. "I've got enough of my own!" So we have, and more than enough; but if we made other folk's sorrows our own as well, the miracle would happen which has been wrought in innumerable lives, the double load would be more tolerable than either of the single loads, and the yoke would become easy and the burden light.

At any rate, when we add the fire of another man's suffering to our own, there is One in the fire "like unto the Son of man," and in that strong controlling Presence "the fire shall not kindle upon thee to destroy." And, at any rate again, when we sorrow with another's sorrow, we are drinking the cup of the Lord, and we enter into "the fellowship of His sufferings."

We can drink that cup of sympathetic suffering in silence. It does not inevitably demand the clumsy instrument of speech. I remember a saintly woman telling me some time ago how she had gone to call upon another woman, over whose life there had suddenly fallen the cold shadow of a benumbing grief. "I just held her hand, and said nothing, and we both wept!"

And when our visitor told me the story, I called to mind how, when those premonitory symptoms occurred which periodically threatened mental darkness to Mary Lamb, she and her brother, Charles Lamb, would go in the early morning, or in the late night, speechless and weeping, over the desolate way that led to the asylum. They said nothing to each other; they just walked the gloomy way, hand in hand. I care little just now what his creed was; I say that when Charles Lamb gave his sorely afflicted sister the hand of a silent but bleeding sympathy he was lifting to his lips the bitter goblet from the table of his Lord; he entered into "the fellowship of His sufferings."

Now I think we are born with an adequate equipment for sharing the sufferings of our fellows. Our very birthright includes a sensitiveness to another's woes. A little child instinctively discerns the shadow, and its tears fall in ready sympathy. But as we grow older, we trifle with this precious inheritance. We waste our substance. We pervert and prostitute our emotional wealth. We are moved, but we do not move; we have a gracious impulse, but we give it no way; and what happens? The waters of unfulfilled emotion congeal into frost, and the very ministers of intended service become the friends of a severer alienation.

That is the peril of novels; they excite an emotion which frequently reacts in petrifying power. And that is the peril of theatres. And that is the peril of sermons! And that is the peril of grace! "It is a savour of life unto life, or of death unto death." Aye, in these high places of emotion fire can become frost, and the emotion which does not issue in practical ministry freezes and binds the very life in which it was born. And so we leave our childhood behind, our endowment becomes our bane, we cease to be able to enter into the sufferings of Christ — and the Saviour suffers alone.

But "blessed are they that mourn," who have not lost their capacity of a weeping and helpful sympathy. Aye, thrice blessed are they who in their prime retain the heart of a little child, who can weep with them that weep, who tread the winepress with the Saviour and enter into "the fellowship of His sufferings."

And, last, in this apostolic ambition to have all things in common, we can enter into the fellowship of our Saviour's sufferings by the all-complete surrender of ourselves to the service of our fellowmen. Our Lord served other people to the point of physical weakness and exhaustion, and even unto death. Our service too frequently ends where bloodletting begins. We stop short of the promise of fertility. "The blood of the martyrs is the seed of the Church." Yes, and the blood of the servant fertilizes the field of his service. "Ye have not yet resisted unto blood!"

And it is just at that point of resistance that we begin to win. It is just when our service becomes costly that it begins to pay. Life becomes contagious when it becomes sacrificial. Our work begins to tell when the workman is content to suffer; when he persists even unto blood.

But is it not true that for many of us our service ends just when we reach the bitter cup? "Are ye able to drink the cup that I drink of?" No, we are not able, and when our work and service become bitter, we give it up. "From that day" — Calvary in sight — "many of His disciples turned back, and walked no more with Him." That teacher in the school—where is he now? Oh, he got tired of it! Which just means that he was not able to go on when to go on drew blood; he could not enter into "the fellowship of the sufferings."

And that is our pitiable mood. So long as there is no drain, we can persist; when there is a demand for the veins to be opened, we retire. And so we miss the best of the feast. For they who take into their hands the goblet of bitterness, humbly saying, "If it be possible, let this cup pass from me: nevertheless, not my will, but Thine be done," will find that by that bitter draught they attain into a spiritual kinship and companionship which is infinite compensation, and even in their sorrow and weariness "the joy of the Lord is their strength."

And so just one word from old Samuel Rutherford, from a letter he wrote to John Kennedy: "ye contracted with Christ, I hope, when first ye began to follow Him, that ye would bear His Cross. Fulfill your part of the contract with patience, and break not to Jesus Christ. . . Be honest, brother, in your bargaining with Him. . . . Forward, brother, and lose not your grips. . . . In the strength of Jesus, dispatch your business!"

CHAPTER FIVE

Through Gethsemane to Olivet

"Then came to Him the mother of the sons of Zebedee, with her sons, worshipping Him, and asking a certain thing of Him" — Matthew 20:20

"Then came"! And what was the particular time which was assumed to be so favourable to the quest? What was the psychological moment? What says the context, for the context so frequently sheds a lurid or interpreting light upon the text? "And as Jesus was going up to Jerusalem, He took the twelve disciples apart, and on the way he said unto them, Behold, we go up to Jerusalem; and the Son of man shall be delivered unto the chief priests and scribes; and they shall condemn Him to death, and shall deliver Him unto the Gentiles to mock, and to scourge, and to crucify; and the third day He shall be raised up."

The narrative is darkening into twilight and night; the heavens are becoming overspread and there loom the approaching presences of betrayal and condemnation and crucifixion. Surely, in such awful midnight, all petty and frivolous thought will be upheaved as by the convulsions of an earthquake! Surely, all trifling purposes will be enlarged by a solemn wonder! Surely, all hot and feverish ambition will be cooled and transfigured into sacred pity and awe! "Then came to Him the mother of the sons of Zebedee, with her sons . . . asking a certain thing of Him."

In a moment of austere sorrow private ambition became obtrusive! We must not assume that these men and their mother had been unimpressed by the master's sad and mysterious speech. I would rather assume that they had shared the general depression, and had been subdued into tender seriousness and tears. But would not the assumption make the association altogether violent and unnatural?

Natural or unnatural, I find many interpreting analogies in my own experience. It is amazing how speedily a settled temper can stain through a new impression and obliterate it. It is marvelous with what strength a dominant purpose can break through a temporary emotion and subdue and destroy it. How often laughter walks just at the heels of tears! How frequently frivolity pitches its tents in the very precincts of the sanctuary!

It is almost incredible what subjects men can discuss when they are returning from a funeral. We gaze into a cold grave, and the wells of emotion are all at the flow; but within thirty minutes our thoughts have regained detachment, and our speech is busy with private or public affairs. Our minds and hearts can be deeply ploughed by the sharp, powerful share of public worship, but, almost before we reach the doors of the sanctuary, the drifting sands of the world are about us again, and the furrows are filled and obscured.

I am not launching an indictment; I am only illustrating an apparently violent conjunction. The old association has its modern analogies, and I am therefore not surprised that this sad and burdensome saying of the Lord should be immediately linked with the request of selfish and vaunting ambition. "Then came to him the mother of the sons of Zebedee, with her sons . . . asking a certain thing of Him."

Now, who were the petitioners? Matthew records that the petition was offered by the mother. In the Gospel of Mark, James and John are reported as making the appeal. The probability is that all three engaged in the supplication, and what one seemed to lack in urgency was supplied by the others.

It does not require a fanciful imagination to recreate some of the preliminary conditions which preceded this open request. The incident here narrated is the culmination of a plot; it is the efflorescence of assiduous culture. Behind this public stage there are domestic conspiracies which it is not difficult to recall. Salome and her two sons, James and John, have often discussed the sons' prospects in the coming kingdom, and many a time, at the end of a day's fellowship with the Master, they have sat late into the night, and even to the cockcrow, considering eligible places in the new dominion.

"You are not half pushing enough," said Salome to her brawny fisherman sons, "your hesitancy will be your undoing! Your silence will be misinterpreted; your very reserve will be counted as indifference! Hangers-back will be regarded as hangers-on, and in the day of dignities you will be nowhere near the throne!

"There's Peter, now, he is never far away from the front, and I've seen the Master cast many a favouring eye upon him! And Nathanael, too, seems to be deep in His confidence, for often have I marked them in long and serious conversation! Judas has even received preliminary office, for already he has been appointed treasurer to the growing band! And then there's Matthew, a skilled man of affairs, with expert understanding of many things, and versed in the ways and mysteries of government! There are a dozen available men, and available offices will not be plentiful, and men like Judas will lose nothing for the asking. Pluck up, my sons, and assert your eagerness!"

And so these two sons often retired to rest, with purpose matured, with their decision made, and they fell asleep dreaming of principalities and powers and exalted offices next to a throne. But in the cooler morning, reserve returned, and the flowing purpose congealed again into rigid reluctance. And I cannot but think that oftentimes they sought to throw the task upon their mother, urging that such a request would come with far more force from her.

"No one can compete with your influence," they said: "you are sister to Mary, His mother, and you can reckon upon her support, and you can prefer the claims of blood!"

And so, day after day, the conversation would be renewed, and day after day the petition was delayed. But now Jerusalem was coming into sight, the centre of sovereignty and power, where the throne would be established, and the Master's face was set so steadfastly toward it.

"It must be now or never," said Salome, "and it shall be now!" "Then came to Him the mother of the sons of Zebedee, with her sons, worshipping Him, and asking a certain thing of Him. And He saith unto her, What wouldst thou? She said unto Him, Command that these my two sons may sit, one on Thy right hand, and one on Thy left hand, in Thy kingdom."

And, now, let us reverently note the yearning pathos of the Saviour's reply. "And Jesus answered and said, Ye know not what ye ask!" There is little or no rebuke in speech or tone. There is no indignant retort that they are asking amiss; there is only a graciously tender answer that they do not know the content of their own request. He assumes that what they are seeking is near companionship in His sovereignty, and very gently He intimates that they cannot have counted the cost.

"Ye ask for sovereignty alongside Me, that ye might share in My dominion; ye know not what is involved in such sovereignty: ye know not what ye ask! Ye think ye are asking for a garden, but in reality ye are asking for a battlefield, for My gardens are just transformed battlefields; and every owner of a garden has been a warrior on the field. Ye know not what ye ask!"

That is the principle of the Master's teaching. Men ask for exalted summits, as though they were the immediate gift of the Saviour's hand, and they are reached by hard and toilsome roads. The teaching is illustrated upon many planes of desire, apart from the distinctly religious.

"Grant that I may stand upon Mount Olivet, my feet resting at the very secret place of its uplifted and radiant splendour!" Ye know not what ye ask: the fatigue, the toil, the danger, which characterize the road that leads to it. "Grant that I may have the wondrously facile skill of some great instrumentalist, that with perfect ease I may weave and fashion rich and moving harmonies! Let me sit upon the throne of the musical world!" Ye know not what ye ask! The sleepless vigilance, the uncheered rehearsals, the aching drill and discipline; musical sovereignties are reached by very obscure and toilsome stairs.

It is not otherwise when we reason in the realm of the spiritual. "Grant that we may sit with Thee on Thy throne!" In this high region dignities are not doled, nor are laurels distributed to every caller at the gate. In the army of the Lord promotion is not by patronage; it is the gracious heritage of fidelity. We do not wing our way to crowns and sovereignties; step by step we trudge to them. "Thou hast been faithful over a few things, I will make thee ruler." "We must through much tribulation enter into the kingdom."

"Ye know not what ye ask!" Ye are seeking for sovereignties — for moral conquests, for spiritual dominions, for some splendid royalty of the soul: "Are ye able to drink the cup that I am about to drink?" "Between you and a share in the sovereign glories of My kingdom there is a cup to be drunk; are ye able?"

Our Saviour is using a very familiar figure in this of the cup, for a man's cup was just the essential nature of the man's particular lot. A man's cup might be sweet or bitter, good or ill, seized and quaffed with ready delight or drunk with sad reluctance. "Thou anointest my head with oil: my cup runneth over!" And that is a cup we all covet to share.

But these are not the draughts that form the mighty cordials of the soul, and endow it with spiritual force and sovereignty. "Are ye able to drink the cup that I am about to drink?" Can you share My present lot, My sacrifice in thought, in prayer, in compassion and service? Will you share a night upon the hill in ceaseless intercession? Will you weep with Me in Gethsemane, and bear upon your burdened hearts the sins and sorrows of the world? Will you enter into the bitter lots of others, and share their unwelcome draught? You ask for a conquest; well, then, are you ready for a crusade?

That is the clarion call of the Lord. We are not called to easy sovereignties, but to glorious campaigns. That is one of the primary significances of the emblems which lie upon the table at the Lord's Supper. They are the memorials of a superlative sacrifice — a life broken, and spent, and laid down for the redemption of the race. They are the emblems of a glorious inspiration, the emblems of a glorified life that is forever sacrificed, ever willing to spend itself to restore and glorify mankind.

And they are the mysteries and symbols of a magnificent calling, dumb mouths appealing to men to give themselves to a great crusade. For can we look at His broken body, broken in service, and then scheme and scheme to keep our skins entire and save them from being worn and broken in the hard and jagged way of service? And can we gaze upon "the blood of the new covenant," the blood so freely shed, and then immure ourselves in slippered ease, and never shed a drop of our heart's blood for the uplifting of the children of men?

It is to young men that I would appeal, and by God's help I would put speech into the dumb mouths of the emblems: it is a young Saviour — only thirty-three when He was crucified — it is "the young Prince of Glory" appealing to the young men, and in the broken bread claiming their bodies, even though they may be broken in the enterprise, and claiming their very blood, that they, too, may bleed in the holy service.

"Ye know not what ye ask!" How frequently we share these uninformed petitions! We, too, are asking for summits, and the Lord answers our prayer; but it is so unlike the answer we expected, for we find ourselves in heavy and burdensome roads; but these are the first fruits of grace, for they mark the road that leads to the heights. I asked the gardener for a finer hedge, closer in texture, a vesture without raggedness — no hole, no rent or seam. And, oh, what mutilations followed the request, what clippings, what bleedings, what apparent waste! A finer hedge had to be gained through the ministry of sacrifice.

You ask your Lord for sovereign joy. You know not what you ask. Deeper joy is the issue of deeper refinement; and so, instead of immediate joy, the Lord led you into the discipline of severity, that the chords of your soul might be rendered more sensitive, that so to their more delicate responsiveness there might be given more exquisite delight.

You ask for sovereign beauty, spiritual beauty; you ask that "the beauty of the Lord" might be upon you. You know not what you ask; for between you and that sovereignty there lies Gethsemane, with its exhausting but beautifying ministries of intercessory prayer and sacrifice.

You are asking for Heaven, for a sovereign abode in the seats of the blest. You know not what you ask!

> "They climbed the steep ascent of heaven,
> "Through peril, toil, and pain!"

Heaven is the abode of the sacrificial, the gathering place of crusaders; the secret of Heaven's glory is to be found in the glorious characters we have fashioned on the way.

And so the gist of it all is this: thrones are for those who are fit to sit on them; we arrive at our throne when we are ready to rule. Sovereignties come to us in grace and sacrifice. It is well to lift our eyes to the hills, to the sublime human sovereignties which fill the vision in the sacred Word, and then, in the strength of God's blessed grace and love, set out for the difficult climb.

For we have not to wait for our Lord's companionship until we reach a throne; He is with us while we are aspiring to it. He does not wait the warrior's arrival when the battle is over and won; He is with us on the field. Our companionship does not begin at the summit; it begins at the base. It is an interchange of cups from the start, "I will come in and sup with him, and he with Me."

The sons of Zebedee came to the throne, but by ways of which they had never dreamed. "Now about that time Herod the king stretched forth his hands to vex certain of the Church. And he killed James the brother of John with the sword." . . . "Ye shall indeed drink of the cup that I drink of!" James scaled his sovereignty by the bloody slopes of martyrdom. As for John, the evening of his days was a stormy and blood-red sunset, spent in the pains of an exile sustained by the inexpressible fellowship of his Lord.

CHAPTER SIX

The Supper of the Lord

"Ye do proclaim the Lord's death till He come"
— 1 Corinthians 11:26

The Lord's Supper is a permanent memorial of Calvary. It is purposed to keep a stupendous sacrifice in mind, and to prevent it from becoming a neglected commonplace. It is a lowly gateway into a most mysterious place. In its wonderful precincts there is unthinkable bitterness of sorrow. And yet out of the very bitterness there comes sweet bread for the soul. There are tears in its silences, and there is also "joy unspeakable and full of glory." How, then, shall we come to the feast?

Sometimes we have come to the Lord's Supper as though it were a battleground, and we have forgotten the feast. We have come as noisy controversialists, and not as hungry guests. We have contended for spiritual privileges which we have not used. We have been heated, quarrelsome, defiant, and we have gone unblessed away.

And ministers have sometimes been so ensnared by the administrative part of the office that they have altogether forgotten that they were sinners. They have "administered," but they have not received, and when they have left the table there has been no holy glow about their souls, and no taste in their mouth of "the glorious liberty of the children of God."

How, then, shall we come to the feast? Let us come as *impure suppliants*. There is no room here to boast of personal merits, but abundance of room to sing the wonders of redeeming grace. This is no place to exhibit webs of our own weaving; it is rather a place of exchange, where we lay down our defective garments and humbly receive "the best robe" in the Father's house, even "the robe of righteousness and the garment of salvation." The most elaborate garment of the self-made man looks very drab and seedy when set in the light which shines around the table of the Lord.

The best thing we can do is to say nothing about our own clothes, but humbly seek that "wedding garment," which is the gift of the Lord of the feast. "Now Joshua was clothed with filthy garments, and stood before the angel. And he answered and spoke unto those that stood before him, saying, Behold, I have caused thine iniquity to pass from thee, and I will clothe thee with apparel. . . . So they set a fair mitre upon his head, and clothed him with garments; and the angel of the Lord stood by."

How shall we come to the feast? Let us come as *sickly disciples*, whose obedience has been thin and faint. We have been anaemic in His service. There has been an obtrusive want of rich, red blood, and the curious, quizzing world has seen the lack, and has wondered whether we were real kinsmen of the warrior with the "red apparel," or whether our claim is a presumptuous pretense. The only authorized Alpine rope has a red worsted strand running through it from end to end. And the really sealed followers of the Lord are known by their red strand, the blood sign, the red, endless line of sacrifice. A life which shows the wan colour of a selfish worldliness, which has nothing to distinguish it from the children of mammon, cannot claim moral kinship with the Lord, who "laid down His life for

His friends." We need the red strand. "My blood is drink indeed." We come to the table in order that our sickly anaemia may be changed into strong and sacrificial chivalry.

> "We lay in dust life's glory dead,
> And from the ground there blossoms red
> Life that shall endless be!"

And so we come as *unimpressive weaklings*, who in ourselves are devoid of forceful grip, and who lack the splendid virile influence of contagious health. We have too frequently moved about our work as though we had "received the spirit of bondage again to fear," and were strangers to the spirit of "love and of power and of a sound mind."

And, therefore, devils have not trembled when we drew near, and when we have commanded their expulsion they have remained powerful and enthroned. They have laughed at our approach, and had we carefully listened we might have heard the old challenge: "Jesus we know, and Paul we know, but who are ye?" The "voice of the great Eternal" was not in our tone, and so the evil spirit proved himself stronger than the professed disciples of the Lord, and we could not cast him out.

And now we come for the bread of strengthening. And this holy bread, this bread of tears, this bread of affliction, is the food of giants. It endows the soul with "the power of His resurrection," and it transforms the ineffective weakling into a strong son of God, and perfectly equips him as a minister of salvation. We have come from defeat and failure up many a pilgrim road, and from many a clime, and we are now in the guest chamber, where the gracious Host is accustomed to meet weary and disheartened pilgrims, and where he graciously feeds them with "the finest of the wheat."

> "Jesus, Thou joy of loving hearts,
> Thou fount of life, Thou light of men,

From the best bliss that earth imparts
We turn unfilled to Thee again!"

And what will He do with us? What will He do for us?
What will He do in us? Well, first of all, He will *com-
mune* with us. He will whisper again to our hearts the wondrous consolations of the fourteenth of John. He will deliver us
from our distraction, and He will smooth out all wrinkling and
wasteful cares.

"Let not your heart be troubled, neither let it be afraid!"
Have we not experienced this quieting ministry of the feast?
Have we not known the gracious seasons when the real life
forces have begun to move, and the soul has begun to kindle,
and the envious distractions of the world have melted away,
just as the imprisoning ice loosens its grasp in the genial breath
of the spring? "Did not our heart burn within us while He
talked with us by the way?"

And thus, while He communes He will communicate, and
the communication is so marvelously abounding and complete
that we become incorporate with the Lord. The fifteenth of
John shall follow the fourteenth; and when the separating fears
and sins have been washed away and we are clean, we shall
know ourselves to be engrafted into the Vine of Life. And no
figure of speech, be it ever so intimate, can express the close-
ness of the incorporation. But friendship, be it endowed with
feelers and tendrils most exquisite, leaves half the tale untold.
Even wedded bliss, when the union seems fleckless and indissoluble, only dimly reflects the fellowship of the soul and
Christ. The Apostle Paul ransacked human experience for symbols of correspondence and intimacy; but even when he had
used the best and most expressive, he laid down his pen in ut-
ter impotence, despairing ever to shadow forth the marvelous
kinship of the soul whose life is "hid with Christ in God."

And how shall we go away from the feast? We must go *as heralds*. We must "proclaim the Lord's death till He come." The Lord's death! We must go out to vagrant pilgrims, who are painfully following illicit lights, and becoming more and more confused, and we must lead them to this strange, solemn birthplace of eternal life and light and hope.

We must "proclaim the Lord's death!" We must tell our struggling fellows that in that fertile gloom gilt finds its solvent, tears become translucent, and moral infirmity begins to "leap as a hart." Yes, we must leave the table as heralds, and this must be our cry: "Ho, everyone that thirsteth, come ye to the waters, and he that hath no money, come ye, buy and eat; yea, come buy wine and milk without money and without price."

And we must go *as covenanters*. We have taken "the new covenant" in His blood, and the holy sacrament will be fresh upon our lips. And there must be something about us akin to the Scottish Covenanters when they emerged from Greyfriars churchyard, having entered into holy bond and covenant with the Lord. There must be something in our very demeanour telling the world that we have been at a great tryst, and our lives must be gravely, grandly quiet, confident in the glorious Ally, with whom the covenant has been made.

There must be nothing dubious in our stride. Our courage must be kingly, as though we have imperial friendships, and as though in very truth we "walk with God." It must be apparent to everybody, in the home, and in the market, and in the street, that we, too, have been "brought again from the dead, . . . through the blood of the everlasting covenant."

As heralds we must go, and as covenanters, and *as crusaders*, too. We must leave the table as the covenanted knights left King Arthur's table, "to ride abroad, redressing human wrong," and to labour for the creation of conditions like unto those whose fair pattern we have seen in the Mount. We may

test the reality of our communion by the vigour of our cru-
sades. We must drink our politics "from the breasts of the
Gospel."

There is a great word in one of Kingsley's letters which
was written when the condition of the people was burdening
him with its ever-deepening tragedy, and when his spirit was
being tortured with the sense of accumulated degradations.
And this is what he wrote:

"If I had not had the communion at church today to tell me
that Jesus *does* reign, I should have blasphemed in my heart, I
think, and said, `The devil is king!'" But he left the feast, he
assures us, braced and strengthened, and with "a wild longing
to do something for his fellow men!" That is it, the power of
the holy blood must be proved in our positive action upon the
kingdom of the night.

> "The Son of God goes forth to war,
> A kingly crown to gain;
> His blood-red banner streams afar,
> Who follows in His train?"

And so let us turn to our feast. The door is open and the
King is near, and blessed are all they that love His appearing.
Let all human ministries veil their faces and stand aside, and
let the soul have undistracted dealings with the Lord.

CHAPTER SEVEN

The Morning Glory

"He is risen" — Matthew 28:6.

And what a sunrise this was after these dark days of disaster and hopeless defeat! It was "like some sweet summer morning after a night of pain." Love had been weeping amid the fallen leaves of her own tender hopes. All her joys were silenced like the songs of wounded birds. Love had been peacefully anticipating the coming of an endless summer, and lo! Here was winter, in dark and merciless severity! The great Lover had seemed to be the very fountain of life, with quickening vitality which nothing could destroy, and yet the fountain had been choked up in Gethsemane and Calvary! "We trusted that it had been He who should have redeemed Israel," but the shining, welcoming pool proved to be only a mirage; hope withered in disillusionment; and the brutal majesty of material force held the entire field.

And so all the disciples were in a mood of deepest and darkest depression. The light had been cut off from their minds. They were in the dark. The taste had gone out of their lives. Everything had become stale and profitless. Simon Peter was gloomy with despondency and haggard with remorse. Two disciples were walking in the twilight to Emmaus, "looking sad," communing about the awful and sudden eclipse in which their hopes had been so miserably quenched.

In every life the light was out. Mary Magdalene started at the "early dawn" to carry spices to the grave, but there was no dawning in her spirit, and the roadway was wet with her tears. Even in the heart of the Magdalene there was no vigil burning, like uncertain candle in a dark and gusty night. No one was anxiously watching on the third day, with eyes intently fixed upon a mysterious east. No; death reigned, and wickedness, and hopelessness, and no one was looking for the morning!

And then came the cry, "He is risen!" The Lord is alive. His tomb is empty! He has shaken off death and its cerements, and He has marched out of the grave! Think of that trumpet note pealing through the late night. Think of that great burning light streaming through the darkness, kindling life after life into blazing hope again — now the Magdalene, now Peter, now John, now the two journeying to Emmaus, now Thomas, until the entire disciple band was a circle of light again. It was an almost unspeakable revolution. "The people that sat in darkness have seen a great light!" "The Lord is risen indeed!"

Now what did the apostles find in the resurrection which made them give it this weighty and unfailing emphasis? What was its practical significance? What did it mean? First of all, it meant this, that *Jesus of Nazareth had been clearly manifested to be the Son of God*. Before this wonderful morning the disciples had been the victims of uncertainty, chilled by cloudy moods of doubt and fear.

But with the resurrection the uncertainty ends. It is not only that the immediate darkness passes, but the troublesome mists are lifted as well, and the Master emerges as the clearly manifested Son of God. "Arise, shine, for thy light is come, and the glory of the Lord is risen upon thee!"

Now, it is with that trumpet note that St. Paul begins his great letter to the Romans. It is well to remember this, because the letter to the Romans is largely concerned with sin and the guilt of sin, and with the sacred ministry of emancipation from its stain and power. And yet, on the very threshold of this mighty book, it is the eternal Sonship of the Lord which is proclaimed, and this in association with the fact of His resurrection from the dead.

Here is the big-lettered placard we meet as soon as we address ourselves to travel this fine and bracing mountain road: "Jesus Christ . . . declared with power to be the Son of God . . . by the resurrection from the dead." Not, you will notice, "declared to be the Son of God with power"; the power belongs to the declaration, the proclamation, the trumpet.

Before the Easter morn the trumpet had seemed to the apostles to give an uncertain sound; there was either a trembling in its notes or a trembling in their ears; but now, with the resurrection, all uncertainty had gone, and the trumpet rang out its glorious blast, firm and rich and clear. "Declared with power to be the Son of God by the resurrection from the dead!"

What else did it mean? *In the power of the resurrection the apostles saw a vast reservoir of spiritual energy for the quickening and emancipation of the race.* This was their reasoning and their faith, that the Lord, who had emerged from the grave, and had thereby vanquished death, had the power to vanquish all death, whether it enthroned itself in body, mind, or soul. This was their faith, as this was their evangel, that in Christ we, too, can rise out of death into newness of life, that, just as He walked out of that tomb, we, too, can walk out of the grave and graveyard of our own corrupt past, and in vigour and sweetness of being become alive unto God.

> "I hold it true with him who sings
> To one clear harp in diverse tones,
> That men may rise on steppingstones
> Of their dead selves to higher things!"

Ay, but those lines omit the evangel. It is true that man can take his own dead self, and stand upon it, and use it as a step into a larger life of blessedness and sacrifice, but the energy wherewith to rise upon the dead self is only to be found in "the power of the resurrection."

That is Paul's gospel, and there is no other. We rise with Christ, we are risen with Christ. Because of the Lord's Easter morn we may pass out of our three days of death and corruption, and may rise to the "higher things," and have our own Eastertide "in heavenly places in Christ Jesus." That is what the apostles found in the resurrection — vitality enough to quicken all the dead, whether the corruption be in body or in soul. "In Christ shall all be made alive."

And surely we have a wonderful symbolism of all this in the mystic movements of the springtime. If anyone would be besieged by suggestions of the resurrection, let him look about in garden and in field, and he will see the quickening glory. Spring is ever a gracious time to me. Never do I so intensely feel the pressure of the quickening Spirit as when I see the black hedgerows bursting with their flooding life into green and tender leaf. Never do I so realize the surging, encompassing energy of God's resurrection communion when the dominion of winter is breaking and the time of the singing of birds is come. "In Christ shall all be made alive!"

I would have the resurrection power flow into my dead affections, and make them bud in tender sympathies, and gentle courtesies, and all the exquisite graces of the heart of my Lord. And I would have the resurrection power pervade my dead conscience, and make it act with hallowed sensitiveness, with fine scrupulous feeling of the sacred and the profane. And I would have the resurrection power possess my mind, and make it fertile in noble ideals, in holy purpose, and in chivalrous resolution.

Wherever there is death where there ought to be life, let there come an Easter dawning and the springtide of our God. And that possibility is just the apostolic evangel, and it is born in the light and joy of the resurrection of our Lord. Again and again I would say, "In Christ shall all be made alive!" "Verily, verily, I say unto you, the hour is coming and now is, when the dead shall hear the voice of the Son of God: and they that hear shall live." "Because He lives, we shall live also!"

And, last, to the early apostles the resurrection had this further significance, *that in it right was manifested as the ultimate might.* It had seemed to the apostles as though the truth had been defeated, that it had been overwhelmed by hordes of wickedness, and that amid the laughter and ribaldry of its foes it had sunk in complete and final disaster.

But on the Easter morn the truth emerged again. It snapped the cerements of the grave, and reappeared almost before the laughter of the enemy had ceased. "Vain the stone, the watch, the seal!" "Truth crushed to earth shall rise again!"

I say that the apostles laid hold of this as one of the primary significances of the resurrection, the vital tenacity of the truth, the indestructibility of the right, its sure and certain resurrection. If we cannot permanently bury the Christ, we cannot permanently bury the Christlike; if One emerged from His temporary grave, so assuredly will the other. Right is the ultimate might, and all the forces of Hell cannot gainsay it.

It may seem at times as though truth is a frail and fragile creature, a tender presence in a tempestuous day, and men may take her, and scourge her, and crucify her, and bury her in a sealed and guarded grave; but, as surely as right is right and God is God, that buried frailty shall reappear in invincible majesty, and shall incontestably dominate and command the affairs of men.

That is apostolic teaching; and, therefore, written in this faith we have that wonderful ending to Paul's great resurrection chapter in his letter to the Corinthians. Have we marked its culmination? "Wherefore," he says, in the closing verse, when he has just taunted the beaten forces of death and the grave, and sang anew the praises of the Lord, "wherefore, my beloved brethren, be ye steadfast, unmoveable, always abounding in the work of the Lord, *forasmuch as ye know that your labour is not in vain in the Lord.*" Do we mark the force of the succession? He seems to say, "Your Lord emerged from the grave in irresistible strength and glory. There were no bonds strong enough to hold Him. He broke them all like tender threads. There was no grave mighty enough to imprison the truth; all the stones were rolled away!

So shall it be with the truth in our life and service. It shall not go under in endless defeat. Our strength shall not be spent for nought, precious water easily spilt upon the ground. Every bit of truth shall live, every bit of chivalrous service shall abide for ever." "Wherefore, be ye steadfast, unmoveable."; go on living the truth, speaking and doing the truth, even though immediate circumstances crush you like a juggernaut — go on — there is resurrection power in the truth, and it shall reappear and surely conquer, and your labour shall "not be in vain in the Lord."

And so it is true, what we learned in childhood, for the Easter morn confirms it, "Kind words can never die, no, never die!" And so it is true what is said by Oliver Wendell Holmes, "Truth gets well if she is run over by a locomotive, while error dies if she scratches her finger."

> "Truth crushed to earth will rise again,
> The eternal years of God are hers,
> But error wounded, writhes with pain,
> And dies amid her worshippers."

"He is risen!" And in our Lord's resurrection is the pledge of the resurrection of all that shares His nature.

THE

PASSION

FOR

SOULS

THE PASSION FOR SOULS

J. H. Jowett, M.A.,D.D.

Seven sermons on the themes tenderness, watchfulness, companionship, rest and vision of the Apostle Paul's passion for human souls. This little volume shows Mr. Jowett's keen, reverent insight at its best.

CHAPTER 1

The Disciple's Theme

*"Unto me, who am less than the least of all saints,
was this grace given, to preach unto the Gentiles
the unsearchable riches of Christ" — Ephesians 3:8*

Mark how the apostle describes the evangel—"the un-searchable riches of Christ!" It suggests the figure of a man standing, with uplifted hands, in a posture of great amaze-ment, before continuous revelations of immeasurable and un-speakable glory. In whatever way he turns, the splendour confronts him! It is not a single highway of enrichment. There are side-ways, byways, turnings here and there, labyrinthine paths and recesses, and all of them abounding in unsuspected jewels of grace. It is as if a miner, working away at the pri-mary vein of ore, should continually discover equally precious veins stretching out on every side, and overwhelming him in rich embarrassment. It is as if a little child, gathering the wild sweet heather at the fringe of the road, should lift his eyes and catch sight of the purple glory of a boundless moor. "The unsearchable riches of Christ!" It is as if a man were tracking out the confines of a lake, walking its boundaries, and when the circuit were almost complete should discover that it was no lake at all, but an arm of the ocean, and that he was confronted by the immeasurable sea! "The unsearchable riches of Christ!" This sense of amazement is never absent from the apostle's life and writings. His wonder grows by what it feeds on. Today's surprise almost makes yesterday's wonder a commonplace. Again and again he checks himself, and stops the march of his argument, as the glory breathes upon him the new freshness of the morning. You know how the familiar paean runs. "According to the riches of His grace." "That He would grant you, according to the riches of His glory." "God shall supply all your need according to His riches in glory by Christ Jesus." "The riches of the glory of this mystery among the Gentiles." "The same Lord over all is rich unto all that call upon Him." "In everything ye are enriched in Him." "The exceeding riches of His grace." His thought is overwhelmed. He is dazzled by the splendour. Speech is useless. Description is impossible. He just breaks out in awed and exultant exclamation. "O, the depth of the riches both of the wisdom and knowledge of God!" The riches are " unsearchable," untrackable, "beyond all knowledge and all thought."

But now, to the Apostle Paul, these "unsearchable riches" are not merely the subjects of contemplation, they are objects of appropriation. This ideal wealth is usable glory, usable for the enrichment of the race. The "unsearchable riches" fit themselves into every possible condition of human poverty and need. The ocean of grace flows about the shore of common life, into all its distresses and gaping wants, and it fills every crack and crevice to the full. That is the sublime confidence of the Apostle Paul. He stands before all the desert places in human life, the mere cinder- heaps, the men and the women with burnt-out enthusiasms and affections, and he boldly proclaims their possible enrichment. He stands before sin, and proclaims that sin can be destroyed. He stands before sorrow, and proclaims that sorrow can be transfigured. He stands before the broken and perverted relationships of men, and proclaims that they can all be rectified. And all this in the strength of "the unsearchable riches of

Christ!" To this man the wealth is realizable, and can be applied to the removal of all the deepest needs of men. Let us fasten our attention here for a little while, in the contemplation of this man's amazing confidence in the triumphant powers of grace.

He stands before sin and proclaims its possible destruction. It is not only that he proclaims the general ministry of pardon and the general removal of sin. He finds his special delight in specializing the ministry, and in proclaiming the all-sufficiency of redeeming grace in its relationship to the worst. There is about him the fearlessness of a man who knows that his evangel is that of a redemption which cannot possibly fail. Turn to those gloomy catalogues which are found here and there in his epistles, long appalling lists of human depravity and human need, and from these estimate his glowing confidence in the powers of redeeming grace. Here is such a list:—"Fornicators, idolaters, adulterers, effeminate, abusers of themselves with men, thieves, covetous, drunkards, revilers, extortioners." Such were some of the foul issues upon which the saving energies of grace were to be brought. And then he adds—"And such were some of you. But ye were washed!" And when the Apostle uses the word "washed" he suggests more than the washing out of an old sin, he means the removal of an old affection; more than the removal of a pimple, he means the purifying of the blood; more than the cancelling of guilt, he means the transformation of desire. Such was this man's belief in the saving ministry of divine grace. Do we share his confidence? Do we speak with the same unshaken assurance, or do we stagger through unbelief? Does our speech tremble with hesitancy and indecision? If we had here a company of men and women whose condition might well place them in one of the catalogues of the Apostle Paul, could we address to them an evangel of untroubled assurance, and would our tones have that savour of persuasion which would make our message believed? What could we tell them with firm and illumined convictions? Could we tell them that the cinder-heaps can be made into gardens, and that the desert can be made to rejoice and blossom as the rose? I say, should we stagger in the presence of the worst, or should we triumphantly exult in the power of Christ's salvation?

It has always been characteristic of great soul-winners that, in the strength of the unsearchable riches of Christ, they have proclaimed the possible enrichment and ennoblement of the most debased. John Wesley appeared to take almost a pride in recounting and describing the appalling ruin and defilement of mankind, that he might then glory in all-sufficient power of redeeming grace. "I preached at Bath. Some of the rich and great were present, to whom, as to the rest, I declared with all plainness of speech, (1) That by nature they were all children of wrath. (2) That all their natural tempers were corrupted and abominable.... One of my hearers, my Lord _____, stayed very impatiently until I came to the middle of my fourth head. Then, starting up, he said, 'Tis hot! 'tis very hot,' and got downstairs as fast as he could." My Lord _____ should have stayed a little longer, for John Wesley's analysis of depravity and of human need was only and always the preface to the introduction of the glories of the unsearchable riches of Christ. My Lord _____ should have waited until Wesley got to the marrow of his text, "The Son of Man is come to seek and to save that which was lost."

There was a similar sublime confidence in the preaching of Spurgeon. What a magnificent assurance breathes through these words, "The blood of Christ can wash out blasphemy, adultery, fornication, lying, slander, perjury, theft, murder. Though thou hast raked in the very kennels of hell, yet if thou wilt come to Christ and ask mercy He will absolve thee from all sin." That too, I think, is quite Pauline. Henry Drummond has told us that he has sometimes listened to confessions of sin and to stories of ill-living so filthy and so loathsome that he felt when he returned home that he must change his very clothes. And yet to these plague-smitten children Drummond offered with joyful confidence the robe of righteousness and the garment of salvation. We need this confident hope today. Men and women are round about us, will-less, heartless, hopeless, and there is something stimulating and magnetic about a strong man's confident speech. If we proclaim the unsearchable riches of Christ, let us proclaim them with a confidence born of experimental fellowship with the Lord, and with the untrembling assurance that the crown of life can be brought to the most besotted, and the pure white robe to the most defiled.

What else does Paul find in the unsearchable riches of Christ? He finds a gracious ministry for the transfiguration of sorrow. The unsearchable riches of Christ bring most winsome light and heat into the midst of human sorrow and grief. "Our consolations also abound through Christ." Turn where you will, in the life of Paul, into his darker seasons and experiences, and you will find that the sublime and spiritual consolation is shedding its comforting rays. "We rejoice in tribulations also." Who would have expected to find the light burning there? "We sorrow, yet not as others who have no hope." "Not as others!" It is sorrow with the light streaming through it! It is an April shower, mingled sunshine and rain; the hope gleams through tears. The light transfigures what it touches! Even the yew tree in my garden, so sombre and so sullen, shows another face when the sunlight falls upon it. I think I have seen the yew tree smile!

Even pain shows a new face when the glory-light beams upon it. Said Frances Ridley Havergal, that exultant singing spirit, with the frail, shaking, pain-ridden body, "Everybody is so sorry for me except myself." And then she uses the phrase, "I see my pain in the light of Calvary." It is the yew tree with the light upon it! Such is the ministry of the unsearchable riches in the night-time of pain. Professor Elmslie said to one of his dearest friends towards the end of his days, "What people need most is comfort." If that be true, then the sad, tear-stricken, heavy-laden children of men will find their satisfaction only in the unsearchable riches of Christ.

What further discoveries does the Apostle make in the unsearchable riches of Christ? He not only confronts sin and claims that it can be destroyed, and stands before sorrow and claims that it can be transfigured, he stands amid the misunderstandings of men, amid the perversions in the pur-posed order of life, the ugly twists that have been given to fellowships which were ordained to be beautiful and true, and he proclaims their possible rectification in Christ. When Paul wants to bring correcting and enriching forces into hu-man affairs, he seeks the wealthy energy in "the unsearch-able riches of Christ" He finds the ore for all ethical and so-cial enrichments in this vast spiritual deposit. He goes into the home, and seeks the adjustment of the home relation-ships, and the heightening and enrichment of the marriage vow. And by what means does he seek it? By bringing Cal-vary's tree to the very hearthstone, the merits of the bleeding sacrifice to the enrichment of the wedded life. "Husbands, love your wives, as Christ also loved the Church and gave Himself for it" He goes into the domain of labour, and seeks the resetting of the relationships of master and servant. And by what means does he seek it? By seeking the spiritual enrichment of both master and servant in a common commu-nion with the wealth of the blessed Lord. He takes our com-mon intimacies, our familiar contracts, the points where we meet in daily fellowship, and he seeks to transform the touch which carries an ill contagion into a touch which shall be the vehicle of contagious health. And by what means does he seek it? By bringing the Cross to the com-mon life and letting the wealth of that transcendent sacrifice reveal the work of the individual soul. Everywhere the Apos-tle finds in the "unsearchable riches of Christ" life's glorious ideal, and the all- sufficient dynamic by which it is to be attained. Here, then, my brethren, are the " unsearchable riches" of Christ— riches of love, riches of pardon, riches of comfort, riches of health, riches for restoring the sin-scorched wastes of the soul, riches for transfiguring the sullenness of sorrow and pain, and riches for healthily adjusting the perverted relationships of the home, the state and the race. These riches are ours. Every soul is heir to the vast inheritance! The riches are waiting for the claimants! And some, yea, multitudes of our fellows have claimed them, and they are moving about in the humdrum ways of common life with the joyful consciousness of spiritual millionaires. One such man is described by James Smetham. He was a humble member of Smetham's Methodist class-meeting. "He sold a bit of tea... and staggered along in June days with a tendency to hernia, and prayed as if he had a fortune of ten thousand a year, and were the best-off man in the world!" His "bit of tea" and his rupture! But with the consciousness of a spiritual millionaire! "All this," said the old woman to Bishop Burnett, as she held up a crust, "all this and Christ!" These are the folk who have inherited the promises, who have even now inherited the treasures in heaven: and "unto me, who am less than the least of all saints, is this grace given, to preach these unsearchable riches of Christ."

Let me turn, in conclusion, from the disciple's theme to the preacher himself. "Unto me, who am less than the least of all saints." Then the disciple is possessed by a sense of profound humility. "Unto me"—the standing amazement of it, that he should have been chosen, first, to share the wealth, to claim the inheritance, and then to make known his discovery to others. "Unto me, who am less than the least"—he violates grammar, he coins a word which I suppose is used nowhere else. It is not enough for Paul to obtain a word which signifies the least, he wants a place beneath the least —"unto me, who am less than the least"—such a word does he require in order to express his sense of his own unworthiness. "Less than the least." He gazes back; surely I don't misinterpret the Apostle when I say it—he gazes back upon the days of his alienation, upon the days when he was deriding and scorning the supposed riches of his Master's kingdom. Again and again, in places where I least expect it, I find the Apostle turning a powerful and, I think, pain-ridden gaze into those early days when he lived in revolt. If you turn to Romans 16, that collection of miscellanies, a chapter which I suppose we don't often read, which is concerned largely with salutations and the courtesies of common life, you get here and there most vivid glimpses into the consciousness of the Apostle. Here is one: "Salute Andronicus, and Junia, my kinsmen, and my fellow-prisoners who were in Christ before me." Do you feel the sob of it—"who were in Christ before me?" They were serving Him, following Him, proclaiming Him, while I was still a declared and implacable foe; they were in Christ before me. But unto me, less than Andronicus, less than Junia, and less than the least of all, unto me was the grace given. I think we shall have to share it with him—this sense of unworthiness at being called and elected by grace to preach the Gospel. We shall have to enter into controversy even with the old Puritan who said, "I do not quarrel with Paul's language, but I do dispute his right to push me out of my place." "Less than the least," said the Puritan, "is my place." Surely the preacher must sometimes lay down his pen, and pause in the very middle of his preparation, in a sense of extreme wonderment that the condescending Lord should have chosen him to be the vehicle and messenger of eternal grace. The man who feels unworthy will be kept open and receptive towards the fountain. "Why did Jesus choose Judas?" said an inquirer once to Dr. Parker. "I don't know," replied the Doctor, "but I have a bigger mystery still. I cannot make out why He chose me." "Unto me, who am less than the least of all saints was this grace given." I wish I could just read that in the very tone and accent in which I think the Apostle himself would have proclaimed it. I think the early part of it would have to be read almost tremblingly. Mark the mingling of profound humility with the tone of absolute confidence. When the Apostle looked at himself he was filled with shrinkings and timidities, but when he thought about his acceptance and his endowment he was possessed by confident triumph. Whatever shrinking he had about himself, he had no shrinking that he was the elect of God, endowed with the grace of God, in order to proclaim the evangel of God. It was just because he was so perfectly assured of his acceptance and of his vocation that he felt so perfectly unworthy. Did not Cromwell say of George Fox that an enormous sacred self-confidence was not the least of his attainments? I am not quite sure that Oliver Cromwell correctly interpreted George Fox. I would be inclined to withdraw the word "self" and insert the word "God," and then we have got, not only what George Fox ought to be, but what the Apostle Paul was, and what every minister of the Gospel is expected to be in Christ; we are expected to be the children of an enormous God-confidence, we are to be children absolutely assured that we are in communion with Christ, and are even now receptive of His grace.

"Unto me was the grace given." Without that grace there can be no herald, and without that grace there can, therefore, be no evangel. You have heard the old legend of the noble hall, and the horn that hung by the gate waiting for the heir's return; none could blow the horn except the heir to the noble pile. One stranger after another would come and put the horn to his lips, but fail to sound the blast. Then the heir appeared, took the horn down from the gate, blew it, and there came the blast that rang down the valley and wound round the hills. "Unto me was the grace given" to blow the horn; "unto me was the grace given" to preach; and none but the one who has the grace of the heir can blow the horn of the Gospel. Our main work, our supreme work, our work, before which all other pales and becomes dim, is to tell the good news, to go everywhere, letting everybody know about the unsearchable riches of Christ. When Professor Elmslie was dying, he said to his wife, "No man can deny that I have always preached the love of God"; and just before he died he said again, "Kate, God is love, all love. Kate, we will tell everybody that, but especially our own boy —at least, you will—we will tell everybody that; that's my vocation." That is the vocation of the disciple, to tell everybody of the unsearchable riches of Christ.

CHAPTER 2

The Disciple's Sacrifice

"I fill up that which is behind of the afflictions of Christ"
— Colossians 1:24

"I FILL up that which is behind!" Not that the ministry of reconciliation is incomplete. Not that Gethsemane and Calvary have failed. Not that the debt of guilt is only partially paid, and there is now a threatening remnant which demands the sacrifice of human blood. The ministry of atonement is perfected. There is no outstanding debt. "Jesus paid it all." In the one commanding sacrifice for human sin Calvary leaves nothing for you and me to do. In the bundle of the Saviour's sufferings every needful pang was borne.

Bearing shame and scoffing rude,
In my place condemned He stood,
Sealed my pardon with His blood.

I can add nothing to that. There is nothing lacking. The sacrifice is all sufficient.

And yet "I fill up that which is behind of the sufferings of Christ." The sufferings need a herald. A story needs a teller. A gospel requires an evangelist. A finished case demands efficient presentation. The monarch must repeat himself through his ambassadors. The atoning Saviour must express Himself through the ministering Paul. The work of Calvary must proclaim itself in the sacrificial saints. In his own sphere, and in his own degree, Paul must be Christ repeated. As a minister in Greece and Asia Minor Paul must reincarnate the sacrificial spirit of Jerusalem and Galilee. He must "fill up that which is behind in the sufferings of Christ." The suggestion is this—all ministry for the Master must be possessed by the sacrificial spirit of the Master. If Paul is to help in the redemption of Rome he must himself incarnate the death of Calvary. If he is to be a minister of life he must "die daily." "The blood is the life." Without the shedding of blood there is no regenerative toil. Every real lift implies a corresponding strain, and wherever the crooked is made straight "virtue" must go out of the erect. The spirit of Calvary is to be reincarnated in Ephesus and Athens and Rome and London and Birmingham; the sacrificial succession is to be maintained through the ages, and we are to "fill up that which is behind in the sufferings of Christ."

"I fill up that which is behind"! That is not the presumptuous boast of perilous pride; it is the quiet, awed aspiration of privileged fellowship with the Lord. Here is an Apostle, a man who thinks meanly enough of himself, counting himself an abortion, regarding himself as "the least of the apostles, not worthy to be called an apostle," and yet he dares to whisper his own name alongside his Master's, and humbly to associate his own pangs with the sufferings of redemptive love. "I fill up that which is behind of the sufferings of Christ." Is the association permissible? Are the sufferings of Christ and His Apostles complementary, and are they profoundly cooperative in the ministry of salvation? Dare we proclaim them together?

Here is an association. "In all their afflictions He was afflicted." "Who is weak and I am not weak; who is offended and I burn not?" Is the association alien and uncongenial, or is it altogether legitimate and fitting? "In all their afflictions He was afflicted"—the deep, poignant, passionate sympathy of the Saviour; "Who is weak and I am not weak"— the deep, poignant, passionate sympathy of the ambassador. The kinship in the succession is vital. The daily dying of the Apostle corroborates and drives home the one death of his Lord. The suffering sympathies in Rome perfected the exquisite sensitiveness in Galilee and Jerusalem. The bleeding heart in Rome perfected the ministry of the broken heart upon the Cross. Paul "filled up that which was behind of the sufferings of Christ."

Here, then, is a principle. The gospel of a broken heart demands the ministry of bleeding hearts. If that succession be broken we lose our fellowship with the King. As soon as we cease to bleed we cease to bless. When our sympathy loses its pang we can no longer be the servants of the passion. We no longer "fill up the sufferings of Christ," and not to "fill up" is to paralyze, and to "make the cross of Christ of none effect." Now the apostle was a man of the most vivid and realistic sympathy. "Who is weak and I am not weak?" His sympathy was a perpetuation of the Passion. I am amazed at its intensity and scope. What a broad, exquisite surface of perceptiveness he exposed to the needs and sorrows of the race! Wherever there was a pang it tore the strings of his sensitive heart. Now it is the painful fears and alarms of a runaway slave, and now the dumb, dark agonies of people far away. The Apostle felt as vividly as he thought, and he lived through all he saw. He was being continually aroused by the sighs and cries of his fellow men. He heard a cry from Macedonia, and the pain on the distant shore was reflected in his own life. That is the only recorded voice, but he was hearing them every day, wandering, pain-filled, fear-filled voices, calling out of the night, voices from Corinth, from Athens, from Rome also, and from distant Spain! "Who is weak and I am not weak?" He was exhausted with other folk's exhaustion, and in the heavy burdensomeness he touched the mystery of Gethsemane, and had fellowship with the sufferings of his Lord.

My brethren, are we in this succession? Does the cry of the world's need pierce the heart, and ring even through the fabric of our dreams? Do we "fill up" our Lord's sufferings with our own sufferings, or are we the unsympathetic ministers of a mighty Passion? I am amazed how easily I become callous. I am ashamed how small and insensitive is the surface which I present to the needs and sorrows of the world. I so easily become enwrapped in the soft wool of self-indulgency, and the cries from far and near cannot reach my easeful soul. "Why do you wish to return?" I asked a noble young missionary who had been invalided home: "Why do you wish to return?" "Because I can't sleep for thinking of them!" But, my brethren, except when I spend a day with my Lord, the trend of my life is quite another way. I cannot think about them because I am so inclined to sleep! A benumbment settles down upon my spirit, and the pangs of the world awake no corresponding sympathy. I can take my newspaper, which is ofttimes a veritable cup-full of horrors, and I can peruse it at the breakfast table, and it does not add a single tang to my feast. I wonder if one who is so unmoved can ever be a servant of the suffering Lord!

Here in my newspaper is the long, small-typed casualty list from the seat of war; or here is half a column of the crimes and misdemeanours of my city; or here is a couple of columns descriptive of the hot and frantic doings of the racecourse; or here is a small corner paragraph telling me about some massacres in China; or here are two little hidden lines saying that a man named James Chalmers has been murdered in New Guinea! And I can read it all while I take my breakfast, and the dark record does not haunt the day with the mingled wails of the orphaned and the damned. My brethren, I do not know how any Christian service is to be fruitful if the servant is not primarily baptized in the spirit of a suffering compassion. We can never heal the needs we do not feel. Tearless hearts can never be the heralds of the Passion. We must pity if we would redeem. We must bleed if we would be the ministers of the saving blood. We must perfect by our passion the Passion of the Lord, and by our own suffering sympathies we must "fill up that which is behind in the sufferings of Christ." "Put on, therefore, as God's elect, a heart of compassion."

Here is another association. Can we find a vital kinship? "He offered up prayers and supplications with strong crying and tears." So far the Master. "I would have you know how greatly I agonize for you." So far the Apostle. The Saviour prayed "with strong crying and tears"; His Apostle "agonized" in intercession! Is the association legitimate? Did not the agony at Rome "fill up" the "strong cryings" at Jerusalem? Does not the interceding Apostle enter into the fellowship of his Master's sufferings, and perfect that "which is behind"? The intercession in Rome is akin to the intercession in Jerusalem, and both are affairs of blood. If the prayer of the disciple is to "fill up" the intercession of the Master, the disciple's prayer must be stricken with much crying and many tears. The ministers of Calvary must supplicate in bloody sweat, and their intercession must often touch the point of agony. If we pray in cold blood we are no longer the ministers of the Cross. True intercession is a sacrifice, a bleeding sacrifice, a perpetuation of Calvary, a "filling up" of the sufferings of Christ. St. Catherine told a friend that the anguish which she experienced, in the realization of the sufferings of Christ, was greatest at the moment when she was pleading for the salvation of others. "Promise me that Thou wilt save them!" she cried, and stretching forth her right hand to Jesus, she again implored in agony, "Promise me, dear Lord, that Thou wilt save them. O give me a token that Thou wilt." Then her Lord seemed to clasp her out-stretched hand in His, and to give her the promise, and she felt a piercing pain as though a nail had been driven through the palm. I think I know the meaning of the mystic experi-ence. She had become so absolutely one with the interceding Saviour that she entered into the fellowship of His cruci-fixion. Her prayers were red with sacrifice, and she felt the grasp of the pierced hand.

My brethren, this is the ministry which the Master owns, the agonized yearnings which perfect the sufferings of His own intercession. And we in the succession? Do our prayers bleed? Have we felt the painful fellowship of the pierced hand? I am so often ashamed of my prayers. They so fre-quently cost me nothing; they shed no blood. I am amazed at the grace and condescension of my Lord that He confers any fruitfulness upon my superficial pains. I think of David Brainerd—I think of his magnificent ministry among the In-dians, whole tribes being swayed by the evangel of the Saviour's love. I wonder at the secret, and the secret stands revealed. Gethsemane had its pale reflection in Susquahan-nah, and the "strong-crying" Saviour had a fellow labourer in His agonizing saint. Let me give you a few words from his journal, after one hundred and fifty years still wet with the hot tears of his supplications and prayers: "I think my soul was never so drawn out in intercession for others as it has been this night; I hardly ever so longed to live to God, and to be altogether devoted to Him; I wanted to wear out my life for Him." "I wrestled for the ingathering of souls, for multi-tudes of poor souls, personally, in many distant places. I was in such an agony, from sun half-an-hour high till near dark, that I was wet all over with sweat; but O, my dear Lord did sweat blood for such poor souls: I longed for more com-passion." Mark the words, "I was in such an agony from sun half-an-hour high till near dark!" May we do what David Brainerd would not do, may we reverently whisper the word side by side with another and a greater word, "And being in an agony He prayed more earnestly." I say, was not Susquahannah a faint echo of Gethsemane, and was not David Brainerd filling up "that which was behind in the sufferings of Christ?" Brethren, all vital intercession makes a draught upon a man's vitality. Real supplication leaves us tired and spent. Why the Apostle Paul, when he wishes to express the poignancy of his yearning intercession for the souls of men, does not hesitate to lay hold of the pangs of labour to give it adequate interpretation. "Ye remember, brethren, our travail." "My little children, of whom I travail in birth again till Christ be formed in you." Again I say, it was only the echo of a stronger word, "He shall see of the travail of His soul and shall be satisfied." Are we in the succession? Is intercession with us a travail, or is it a playtime, a recreation, the least exacting of all things, an exercise in which there is neither labour nor blood? "The blood is the life." Bloodless intercession is dead. It is only the man whose prayer is a vital expenditure, a sacrifice, who holds fellowship with Calvary, and "fills up that which is behind in the sufferings of Christ."

Here is another association. Is it legitimate? "Master, the Jews of late sought to stone Thee, and goest Thou thither again?" "Having stoned Paul" (at Lystra) "they drew him out of the city supposing he had been dead." And Paul "returned again to Lystra!" Back to the stones! Is that in the succession? Is not the Apostle the complement of his Master? Is he not doing in Lystra what his Master did in Judaea? Is he not filling up "that which was behind of the sufferings of Christ?" Back to the stones! "Master, the Jews of late sought to stone Thee, and goest Thou thither again?" The Boxers of late sought to decimate thee, poor little flock, and goest thou thither again? The New Guineans have butchered thy Chalmers and thy Tompkins, and goest thou thither again? Mongolia has swallowed thy men and thy treasure, and its prejudice and its suspicions appear unmoved, and goest thou thither again? Thou halt been tiring thyself for years, seeking to redeem this man and that man, and he treats thee with indifference and contempt, and goest thou thither again? My brethren, are we familiar with the road that leads back to the stones? It was familiar to the Apostle Paul, and when he trod the heavy way he entered the fellowship of his Master's pains, and knew that he "filled out that which was behind of the sufferings" of his Lord. To go again and face the stones is to perpetuate the spirit of the Man who "set His face steadfastly to go to Jerusalem," even though it meant derision, desertion, and the Cross. We never really know our Master until we kneel and toil among the driving stones. Only as we experience the "fellowship of His sufferings can we know the power of His resurrection." There is a sentence in David Hill's biography—that rare, gentle, refined spirit, who moved like a fragrance in his little part of China —a sentence which has burned itself into the very marrow of my mind. Disorder had broken out, and one of the rioters seized a huge splinter of a smashed door and gave him a terrific blow on the wrist, almost breaking his arm. And how is it all referred to? "There is a deep joy in actually suffering physical violence for Christ's sake." That is all! It is a strange combination of words—suffering, violence, joy! And yet I remember the evangel of the Apostle, "If we suffer with Him we shall also reign with Him," and I cannot forget that the epistle which has much to say about tribulation and loss, has most to say about rejoicing! "As the sufferings of Christ abound in us, so our consolation also aboundeth through Christ." "Out of the eater comes forth meat." These men did not shrink from the labour when the stones began to fly. Rebuff was an invitation to return! The strength of opposition acted upon them like an inspiration. Have you ever noticed that magnificent turn which the Apostle gives to a certain passage in his second letter to the Corinthians? "I will tarry at Ephesus... for a great door and effectual is opened unto me, and *there are many adversaries!*" "There are many adversaries... I will tarry!" The majestic opposition constitutes a reason to remain! "There are many adversaries;" I will hold on! My brethren, that is the martyr's road, and he who treads that way lives the martyr's life, and even though he do not die the martyr's death he shall have the martyr's crown. Back to the stones! "It is the way the Master went," and to be found in that way is to perpetuate the sacrificial spirit, and to "fill up that which is behind of the sufferings of Christ."

To be, therefore, in the sacrificial succession, our sympathy must be a passion, our intercession must be a groaning, our beneficence must be a sacrifice, and our service must be a martyrdom. In everything there must be the shedding of blood. How can we attain unto it? What is the secret of the sacrificial life? It is here. The men and the women who willingly and joyfully share the fellowship of Christ's sufferings are vividly conscious of the unspeakable reality of their own personal redemption. They never forget the pit out of which they have been d u g, and they never lose the remembrance of the grace that saved them. "He loved me, and gave Himself for me;" *therefore*, "I glory in tribulation!" "by the grace of God I am what I am;" *therefore* "I will very gladly spend and be spent!" The insertion of the *"therefore"* is not illegitimate: it is the implied conjunction which reveals the secret of the sacrificial life. When Henry Martin reached the shores of India he made this entry in his journal, "I desire to burn out for my God," and at the end of the far-off years the secret of his grand enthusiasm stood openly revealed. "Look at me," he said to those about him as he was dying—"Look at me, the vilest of sinners, but saved by grace! Amazing that I can be saved!" It was that amazement, wondering all through his years, that made him such a fountain of sacrificial energy in the service of his Lord.

My brethren, are we in the succession? Are we shedding our blood? Are we filling up "that which is behind in the sufferings of Christ?" They are doing it among the heathen. It was done in Uganda, when that handful of lads, having been tortured, and their arms cut off, and while they were being slowly burned to death, raised a song of triumph, and praised their Saviour in the fire, "singing till their shrivelled tongues refused to form the sound." They are doing it in China, the little remnant of the decimated Churches gathering here and there upon the very spots of butchery and martyrdom, and renewing their covenant with the Lord. They are "filling up that which is behind of the sufferings of Christ." They are doing it among the missionaries. James Hannington was doing it when he wrote this splendidly heroic word, when he was encountered by tremendous opposition: "I refuse to be disappointed; I will only praise!" James Chalmers was doing it when, after long years of hardship and difficulty, he proclaimed his unalterable choice: "Recall the twenty-one years, give me back all its experience, give me its shipwrecks, give me its standings in the face of death, give it me surrounded with savages with spears and clubs, give it me back again with spears flying about me, with the club knocking me to the ground—give it me back, and I will still be your missionary!" Are we in the succession?

A noble army, men and boys,
The matron and the maid,
Around the Saviour's throne rejoice,
In robes of light arrayed;
They climbed the steep ascent of Heaven
Through peril, toil and pain!
O God, to us may grace be given
To follow in their train.

CHAPTER 3

The Disciple's Tenderness

"And I will betroth thee unto Me forever."
— Hosea 2: 19.

THAT is a tenderly beautiful figure; surely one of the sweetest and most exquisite in God's Word! "I will betroth thee unto Me forever!" The communion of ideal wedlock is used to express the ideal relationship between the soul and its Lord. We are to be married unto the Lord! Look into the heart of it, and see how much the gracious figure reveals.

"I will betroth thee unto Me forever." There is to be a wedding of the soul and its Saviour, of the nation and its King. To bring that wedding about is the aim and purpose of every kind and type of Christian ministry. We are to labour to bring souls into marriage-covenant with their Lord. I wish for the present to limit my outlook entirely to the winning of the children, and shall engage your thought to the pertinent problem as to how they can be wooed into a marriage-contract with the Lord of glory. What is the kind of wooing that will lead to a wedding?

Let me begin here. I do not think we greatly help the cause of the Lover by proclaiming the remoteness of the

Lover's home. I have never been able to find out what we gain by teaching children the "far-offness" of the Saviour's dwelling.

> There is a happy land
>
> *Far, far away!*

How does that help the wooer?

> *For beyond the clouds and beyond the tomb*
> *It is there, it is there, my child.*

I say, how does that help the wooing? I am afraid that the remoteness of the home tends to create a conception of the remoteness of the Lover; and, if the Lover is away, the wooing will be very mechanical and cold.

> *There's a Friend for little children*
> *Above the bright blue sky.*

That is the only line I don't like in that greatly beloved and very beautiful hymn. In my childhood it helped to make my Saviour an absentee, and He was "above the bright blue sky," when I wanted Him on the near and common earth. I think that we shall perhaps best help the cause of the Wooer if we teach that His home is very near, and that no clouds interpose between us and the place of His abiding.

> *There is a happy land,*
> *Not far away.*

Destroying all sense of remoteness, we must labour to bring the children into the immediate presence of the Lover Himself. How shall we do it? What is there in the child of which we must lay hold? To what shall we make our appeal? Ruskin was never weary of telling us that the two fundamental virtues in childhood are reverence and compassion, the sympathetic perception of another's weakness, and the venerating regard for another's crown. To perceive the sorrows of life, and to maintain a sense of the dignities of life, are two rare and choice endowments; and, when these are exercised upon "the Man of Sorrows," and "the King with many crowns," the issue will be a life of commanding spiritual devotion. But Ruskin's analysis does not altogether, and quite fittingly, serve my purpose here. It is more to my purpose to borrow the familiar line of Wordsworth, for his teaching includes the teaching of Ruskin, and also adds to it —"We live by admiration, hope, and love." In those three attributes a man's personality abides. Gain them, and you win the man! All the three attributes must be regarded in indissoluble union. The quality of each depends upon the presence of all. Strike out one, and you maim and impoverish the rest. There is an imperfect love in which there is no admiration. There is an imperfect admiration in which there is no love. Perfect love admires: perfect admiration loves; and love and admiration are ever associated with the gracious spirit of hopeful aspiration. These three, I say, constitute the very marrow of life—the deep, secret springs of character and conduct. "We live by admiration, hope, and love." To win a child's love, and admiration, and hope, is to grip his entire being, and make conquest of all the powers of his soul. If the great Lover can win these, the wooing will be followed by the wedding. How can we so represent Him, that this triumph shall be won?

We have so to reveal Jesus to the children, that He captivates their love. What shall we reveal to them? Instinctively, I think, we feel that we must let them gaze long at His beauteous simplicity. We must reveal Him handling the lilies; we must strive to make it so real, that the children, with their magnificently realistic imagination, shall feel that they are with Him among the flowers of the field. We must reveal Him watching the graceful flight of the birds of the air, and His peculiarly tender regard for the common sparrow. We must reveal Him pausing to give thought to the hen and her chickens, and His wistful interest in the sheep and the sheepfold. We must reveal Him as the approachable Jesus, with groups of little children clustering about His knees; not bored by them, not too great for their companionship, but lovingly taking them into His arms to bless them; and, if there is some puny weakling among them, giving to that one some special caress and regard. Will these fascinating simplicities, if vividly revealed, be ineffective in awaking the impressionable responsiveness of a little child? Depend upon it, the heart will begin to thrill! But not only His simplicity must we reveal, but His sympathy too! We must whip up our own powers, and seek to clearly depict for the child the great Lover's love for the weak, the defenseless, the unloved, and the abandoned.

But cannot we go further? Must we confine the visions of the children to the simplicities and sympathies of the Lover? Must we just keep to the fireside Jesus, the Jesus of the lilies, the farmyard, and the sheepfold, the good-Samaritan Jesus, binding up the wounds of the bruised and broken? Shall we keep the children in the "green pastures," and by "the still waters," or shall we take them into "the valley of the shadow?" Shall they abide upon the sunny slopes of Galilee, and watch the Lover there, or shall we guide their feet into Gethsemane, and let them gaze on Calvary? Brethren, I will give my own experience; at any rate, it is one man's witness, and represents, I avow, the findings of one who seeks to woo young life into covenant-communion with the Lord. I sometimes take my young people into the garden of Gethsemane and up the hill of Calvary; I do not do it frequently, lest the *via dolorosa* should become a common way, and should be trod with flippant step; but now and again, when I think I dare, I lead them into the shadow of the Passion, and whisper to them hints of the awful mystery! And what do I find? My brethren, I find there is no wooing like that! It is not only for the reprobate, but also for the little child, that in the passion of the Lord there is unbared the infinite love of the Lover. There is no need to be sensational. The sensational is never the parent of fruitful love. Gethsemane was very quiet, and all we need to do is to walk very softly, taking the children with us, and let them gaze upon the Sufferer as He bows amid the olive-groves on that most eventful night. The spiritual appreciativeness of the child will supply the rest. "I thank Thee, O Father... that Thou hast hid these things from the wise and prudent, and hast revealed them unto babes." "Out of the mouths of babes and sucklings hast Thou ordained praise." I say there is no wooing like this! The spiritual marriage contract is most frequently made in Gethsemane and at the Cross. "The love of Christ constraineth me."

"We live by love." By "admiration" too! Our children must not only find in the Lover their Saviour; they must find in Him their Hero too. Say to yourself, "I will so present my Master as a Hero as to woo the adoring homage of my boys." Would you suffer from any lack of matter? Your eyes are closed and sealed if you do not see the. heroic glowing upon every page of the sacred story! His splendid chivalry; His tremendous hatred of all meanness and sin; His magnificent "aloneness" in the night; His strenuous refusal of a popular crown, when the sovereignty would mean compromise with the powers of darkness! Let these be unfolded with the same tremendous effort at vivid realization which we make when we seek to unveil the heroisms of a Cromwell, a Howard, or a Gordon, and our boys and girls will go on their knees before the unveiling with reverent admiration and homage. " Thou art worthy, O Christ, to receive all honour and glory."

Loving! Admiring! These fair dispositions will be assuredly associated with the beautiful genius of hope. The glorious Lord will become the children's bread. Their worship will become their hunger. Their loving will become their longing. Their admiration will become their aspiration. Their faith will become their hope. They will be laid hold of in all the fetters and feelings of personality, and the great Wooer will have won.

What more shall we say about ourselves? Let this be said: while we are employed in wooing do not let us be heedless as to the manner of our living. I know that is a great commonplace, but I know also that it is by the preservation of the commonplace that we maintain the wholeness and sanity of our lives. Those who woo for the Master must be careful how they live. The detection of inconsistency is fatal to the reception of our message. " A child is the most rigid exacter of consistency." "I say" may count for little or nothing. "I know" may count for very little more. " I am" is the incarnation which gives defense and confirmation to the Gospel, and reveals the deputy- wooer in something of the reflected beauty of the glorious Lover Himself. The wooers must themselves be won; and our own conquest must be proved by the brightness and purity of our wedding apparel and the radiant buoyancy of our dispositions. I say the wooers must be in wedding attire, and must be "children of light," children of the morning. "I wonder if there is so much laughter in any other home in England as in ours." So wrote Charles Kingsley in one of his incomparable letters to his wife! That sounds fascinating, captivating, there is the ring of the wedding-bells in the quaint and only partially hidden boast. I do not wonder that this child of the morning was such a mighty wooer for his Lord! Let us beware of a forced seriousness. Let us discriminate between sobriety and melancholy. It was a saying of David Brainerd's that "there is nothing that the devil seems to make so great a handle of as a melancholy humour." Let us distinguish between a wedding and a funeral, and in our wooing let it be the wedding-bells which lend their music to our speech. I confess that in the school-teaching of my early days I think the wooers gave too much prominence to the minor key, and the dirge of melancholy resignation too often displaced the wedding-march of a triumphant walk with God.

When shall we begin the wooing? When I had written that sentence I chanced to lift my eyes from the paper, and I saw a tender fruit-sapling just laden with blossom. At what age may a sapling blossom? At what age may a young life begin to blossom for the King? To revert to my figure—when shall we begin the wooing? Plato said, "The most important part of education is right training in the nursery." And Ruskin said; "When do you suppose the education of a child begins? At six months old it can answer smile with smile, and impatience with impatience." Perhaps we have to begin the wooing even in the speechless years. In the life of the Spirit I believe in early wooings because I believe in early weddings! The wooing and the wedding become increasingly difficult when we pass the age of twelve. As for the wedding itself, the betrothal to the lord, I would have it a very decisive act. It must be a conscious, intelligent consecration. The vow must not be made in thoughtlessness; not in any bewildering and sensational transports. In the rapture there must be the moderating presence of serious and illumined thought. But mind you, the act of decision must be a wedding and not a funeral. It must be serious and yet glad.

I give my heart to Thee,
Saviour Divine.
For Thou art all to me
And I am Thine.
Is there on earth a closer bond than this
That my Beloved's mine and I am His?

CHAPTER 4

The Disciple Watching for Souls

"I will make you fishers of men."— Matt. 4: 19.

I WISH to devote this chapter to the consideration of the serious work of watching for souls. I do not presume to be a teacher who has secrets to unfold; still less can I claim to be an expert in the great vocation. I suppose it is true of all preachers that as we grow older our sense of the inefficiency of our work becomes intensified. The wonder grows that God can accomplish so much with such inadequate implements. One's satisfaction with the evangel deepens with the years; but one is increasingly discontented with the imperfect way in which we present it. No, I do not write as one who is proficient; I am only a blunderer at the best; but I write as one who is honestly desirous of better and more useful equipment. I have often been amused by the headline to the preface in Isaac Walton's *Compleat Angler*. Here is the quaint sentence: "To the reader of this discourse, but especially to the Honest Angler." And in this chapter I conceive myself as writing, not to expert anglers, or even to successful anglers, but to those who are "honest," and who are sincerely desirous to become proficient in their ministry. More than two hundred years ago there was a young probationer in the Church of Scotland named Thomas Boston. He was about to preach before the parish of Simprin. In contemplation of the eventful visit he sat down to meditate and pray. "Reading in secret, my heart was touched with Matt. 4: 19: Follow Me, and I will make you fishers of men.' My soul cried out for the accomplishing of that to me, and I was very desirous to know how I might follow Christ so as to be a fisher of men, and for my own instruction in that point I addressed myself to the consideration of it in that manner." Out of that honest and serious consideration there came that quaint and spiritually profound and suggestive book: "A Soliloquy on the Art of Man-Fishing." All through Thomas Boston's book one feels the fervent intensity of a spirit eager to know the mind of God in the great matter of fishing for souls. Without that passion our enquiry is worthless. " The all-important matter in fishing is to have the desire to learn."

"Now for the art of catching fish, that is to say, how to make a man—that was not—to be an angler by a book; he that undertakes it shall undertake a harder task than Mr. Hales, a most valiant and excellent fencer, who in the printed book called A Private School of Defence,' undertook to teach that art or science, and was laughed at for his labour — not that but many useful things might be learned by that book, but he was laughed at because that art was not to be taught by words. " So says Isaac Walton in his famous book on Angling. It is painfully true. If books would make an angler, I should be the most expert fisher in this neighbourhood. On one of my shelves there is quite a little collection of fishing books, out of which I have been able to borrow many hints and suggestions for my own particular labour. I think I know them fairly well, and in many of their chapters could pass an examination with honours. But in the practical handling of the rod I should come in the rear of the most incompetent. In angling I am a splendid theorist, but useless in practice. Is it not here that we must begin our consideration

of the matter of the ministry of Christ? Books cannot make a preacher; he may find them full of helps, but they are not creators of gifts. They may teach how to make sermons, but they have nothing to do with the creation of prophets. We are made by Christ. "I will make you." We are fashioned in His presence. Every wealthy and fruitful gift for our work is born directly of His own grace and love. Ring out the music of the changing emphasis in this phrase! The promise reveals its treasure as each word is taken in turn and given distinct prominence. " I will make you"; no one else and nothing else can do it. Neither books, nor colleges, nor friends! "I will *make* you"; He will make us just in that secret and mysterious way in which true poetry comes into being. The gift will come as a breath, as an inspiration, as a new creation. " When He ascended on high... He gave gifts unto men." He dropped one gift here, and a commonplace man became a pastor. He dropped another gift there, and the undistinguished became a prophet. He dropped a third gift yonder, and an impotent man became a powerful evangelist. "I will make you fishers of men." But even though the germinal gifts of the preacher are Christ-born and Christ-given, our Lord expects us to reverently and diligently use our minds. He will further fashion and. enrich His gifts through our own alertness. The incipient capacity will be developed by our own intelligent observation and experience. What can we learn which will foster our heaven-born gift? Let us turn to the fisher in natural waters, and see what hints he may give us for the labours in our own sphere. What, then, does the angler say to fishers of men?

Keep out of sight! Mark Guy Pearse is an expert fisher, and rarely does a year pass without his paying a visit to the rivers of Northumberland. And he has more than once laid down what he considers to be the three essential rules for all successful fishing, and concerning which he says, "It is no good trying if you don't mind them. The first rule is this: Keep yourself out of sight. And secondly, keep yourself fur-

ther out of sight. And thirdly, keep yourself further out of
sight!" Mr. Pearse's counsel is confirmed by every fisher. A
notable angler, writing recently in one of our daily papers,
summed up all his advice in what he proclaims a golden max-
im: "Let the trout see the angler and the angler will catch no
trout." Now this is a first essential in the art of man-fishing:
the suppression and eclipse of the preacher. How easily we
become obtrusive! How easily we are tempted into self-ag-
gressive prominence! How prone we are to push ourselves to
the front of our work in quest of fame and praise and glory!
The temptation comes in a hundred different ways. It steals
upon us in the study and spoils our secret labour. It destroys
the efficacy even of the bait that we prepare. It comes upon
us in the pulpit and perverts our workmanship even when we
are in the very midst of our work. The devil secretly whispers
to us in most unctuous flattery: "That was a fine point you
made." And we readily respond to the suggestion. And so the
insidious destruction is wrought. We don't stand aside. If I
may vary my figure, let me say that our function is to draw
aside the curtain and hide ourselves somewhere in its robes.
Let us remember that so soon as our people see the preacher
they will not take his bait. As soon as we become prominent
our Lord is never seen. Keep out of sight!

Cultivate a mood of cheeriness and praise. Here is a bit
of counsel from an old book whose phraseology and spelling
have quite an old-world flavour about them. It is a book on
fishing. The writer is recording the requisite virtues of the angler: "He should not be unskillful in musick, that whensoever
either melancholy, heaviness of his thoughts, or the perturba-
tions of his own fancies, stirreth up sadness in him, he may
remove the same with some godly hymn or anthem, of
which David gives him ample examples." Is that not rather a
far-fetched notion of an angler's equipment? Why should he
require the gift of music? Because, says my author, when the
angler is depressed he cannot throw a light line. When a man
is melancholy his throw will be heavy. When his spirits are

light and exuberant, he will be able to touch the surface of the water with the exquisite delicacy of a passing feather. Can we not apply the counsel to the ministry of preaching? If we come into our pulpits in a depressed and complaining frame of mind, we shall lack the requisite throw. If we are possessed by melancholy we shall catch no fish. And therefore it is well that we, too, should resort to the service of song. We must sing away our depressions and melancholies before we preach the evangel of grace. We must put on "the garment of praise." I frequently consult a book given to me many years ago, and now out of print: "Earnest Christianity," an account of the life and journal of the Rev. James Caughey. There is much in that journal that reminds me of David Brainerd and John Wesley. One day James Caughey was depressed and melancholy, full of lamentation and complaint. There was no music in his spirit and there was no power upon his tongue. He preached, but ineffectively, because his words were not pervaded by the spirit of praise. And then he took to the corrective of prayer and singing. He adopted William Law's counsel, and chanted himself into lightness and buoyancy of heart. He exchanged the "spirit of heaviness for the garment of praise." And now mark the change in the diary: "Easy preaching now. The sword has a new edge, more apt to penetrate; more strength in my soul's arm to lay it round me fearlessly." That is the spirit. We must address ourselves to the great act of preaching in the exuberance which belongs to a thankful and praiseful heart.

Study the fish! George Eliot was once listening to the complaints of some angling friends as they were describing their fruitless day's work. Looking into their empty creels she said: "You should make a deeper study of the subjectivity of the trout." That is a very suggestive word, and pregnant with significance for the fishers in the world of men. We must study the fish that we may find out what will win them for the Lord. All fish cannot be caught by the same bait. We must study the individual prejudices, and habits and tastes.

We must discover what will catch this man and that man, and address ourselves accordingly. I was once passing through a little village in the Lake district, and there was a card in the shop window which gave me more than a passing thought. On the card were a number of artificial flies with this engaging headline: "Flies with which to catch fish in this locality." The shopkeeper had nothing to say about the requirements of the Midlands. He had studied the characteristics of the fish in his own neighbourhood, and he had discovered what bait provided the best allurement. We preachers must do it in our own localities. It was the practice of the Apostle Paul: "To the Jews I became as a Jew that I might gain the Jews." He became "all things to all men that he might gain some." He baited his hook according to the fish he wanted to catch. I don't think we should fish with the same hook for Lydia and the Philippian jailer. It may be that we shall discover that a sermon will never effect the purpose. We may find out that a letter will do infinitely better work. Or it may be that a direct talk may be the requisite constraint. Or, again, it may be that a long conversation, apparently indirect and aimless, but quietly dropping one delicate hint, may win a soul for Christ. Study the fish!

Learn from other fishermen! Other men will never make us fishers, but they may make us better fishers. If we have the rudimentary gift their experience may help to enrich it. Let us turn to the expert fishermen and see if their ways and methods can give us helpful counsel. John Wesley was a great fisher, can we learn anything from him? Dr. Alexander Whyte has told us how he has made a patient and laborious study of John Wesley's journals for the purpose of classifying all the texts upon which the great preacher built his evangel. Is not that a splendid discipline for anyone who wishes to become skillful in the great ministry? What did Wesley preach about? And how did he fit his message to the changing circumstances of his varying spheres? The Salvation Army has a great body of expert fishers. They lack many things, but they catch fish. .How do they do it? We may dislike many of their ways, but what is it in their ministry which enables them to win multitudes for the Lord? What was the secret of Finney and Moody? And what is it about Torrey which constrains the people to become disciples of the Christ? Let us set about this investigation like men who wish to do great business for the Lord. Let us eagerly pick up any hints which these highly endowed and experienced men may be able to give us.

"It is a great matter to take a trout early in your trial. It gives one more heart. It seems to keep one about his business. Otherwise you are apt to fall into unproductive reverie." I know no word more closely applicable to the work of the ministry. If we do not catch men we are in great danger of losing even the desire to catch them. Our purposed activity is in peril of becoming a dream. Let me counsel my fellow preachers in the lay ministry to make up their minds to catch one soul, to go about it day and night until the soul is won. And when they have gained one man for the Master I have then no fear as to what will be their resultant mood. The joy of catching a soul is unspeakable! When we have got one soul we become possessed by the passion for souls. Get one and you will want a crowd I And let me say this further word. Keep a list of the names of the souls you win for the King, and if on any day you are apt to be cast down, and the lightness and buoyancy go out of your spirit, bring out that list and read it over, and let the contemplation of those saved lives set your heart a-singing and inspire you to fresh and more strenuous work. It is a good thing to have lists of the Lord's mercies by which to drive away the clouds in a day of adversity. Let your labour be directed to the immediate catching of men for the Lord. "It is a great matter to take a trout early in your trial."

And now I will close this meditation by offering a suggestion which I obtained from an advertisement in an anglers' paper some time ago. "Now is the time for your old favourite rods to be overhauled and treated with a steel tonic that will not fail to work wonders in the way of renewing their strength." And following this advertisement came this confirmatory testimonial: "I am glad to acknowledge that a very whippy gig-whip of a rod has been converted into a powerful weapon." My hearers will immediately perceive the spiritual significance of the words. There are times when we need the "steel tonic" in order that our poor ministries may be converted into powerful weapons. And, blessed be God, we have the promise of this redemptive work in the very names in which the Holy Spirit is revealed to us. He is called the Renewer, the Reviver, the Restorer of souls, and by His baptism the poorest, weakest agent can be turned into a powerful weapon. "They that wait upon the Lord shall renew their strength." Let us turn to our Lord this very night, and seek for that renewal in the strength of which we shall turn to our work with multiplied possibility, and with perfect assurance of success.

CHAPTER 5

The Disciple's Companion

"Did ye receive the Holy Ghost when ye believed? And they said unto him, Nay, we did not so much as hear whether the Holy Ghost was given" — Acts 19:1-3

"DID ye receive the Holy Ghost when ye believed?" Why did he put the anxious question? Were there some ominous signs of impoverishment which aroused this painful wonder? Did he miss something? He certainly did not suspect the reality and sincerity of their faith. The separation of this little body of twelve men from the mighty drift and popular fashion of Ephesian life was itself an all-sufficient proof that they were moving in the fear of the Lord. And yet to the Apostle's trained and discerning eye there was something lacking! I know not what were the signs which stirred his solicitude. Perhaps it was the large care-lines ploughed so deeply upon their faces. Perhaps it was a certain slow heaviness in their walk, or a certain stale flatness in their intercourse. Perhaps it was a look of defeat in their tired eyes— the expression of exhausted reserves, the lack of exuberance, the want of a swinging and jubilant optimism. Perhaps it was the absence of the bird-note from their religious life. I know not what the signs may have been, but some conspicuous gap yawned before the Apostle's penetrating vision, which prompted him to ask this trembling, searching question, "Did ye receive the Holy Ghost when ye believed?" And the half-spent and wearied souls replied, "Nay, we did not so much as hear whether the Holy Ghost was given!" How imperfect their equipment! How inadequate their resources! They were resisting the day's drift with a quite insufficient endowment. They were endeavouring to counteract and transform the fashion of the world with quite inferior dynamics. I know that mighty dynamics can work along the flimsiest threads, and I know that the heavenly powers can operate through the slenderest faith; but there is an unenlightened, a non-vigilant, a non-expectant attitude of mind which negatives the divine ministry, which impedes the inflow of the divine power, and which reduces the soul to comparative weakness and impoverishment. The day of Pentecost had come; the marvellous promises had been fulfilled; the wonder- ministry had begun; but these disciples were still in the pre-Pentecostal days: they were behind the spiritual times! "We did not so much as hear whether the Holy Ghost was given." And if you would. discover what it means for men to step from pre-Pentecostal dearth to Pentecostal fullness, you must compare the earlier atmosphere of this incident with the atmosphere of its close, and you will find how these weary, labouring men, heavy-footed, heavy-minded, with slow and stammering lips, are transformed into nimble, buoyant, and resourceful servants of the Lord. "The Holy Ghost came upon them, and they spake with the tongues and prophesied."

But what is the relevancy of all this to our own time? The precise lineaments of this incident are not repeated to-day. No such impoverishing ignorance prevails among the modern disciples. We know that the Holy Ghost has been given. We *know*! Ah, I am using a New Testament word, and I must attach to it the wealth of New Testament significance. We may "know," in the way of cognition: a bare act of the intelligence; a merely mental acquisition. And we may "know," in the way of a living fellowship, by the intimate discernments of communion, by the delights and satisfactions of the soul, by real and practical experience. As a matter of cognition, of merely mental enlightenment, we may live in the spacious days of Pentecost; but in daily usage and common experience we may be living in the leaner and straitened days which preceded it. I am deeply persuaded that, judged experimentally by our daily life and practice, much of the mental attitude and spiritual pose of the modern Church is pre-Pentecostal, and that in this thin and immature relationship is to be found the secret of our common weariness and impotence. This is the relevancy of the ancient incident: Do we share their mental temper, their spiritual standpoint, their angle of vision? Are we a little band of pilgrims, laboriously toiling over desert sands, with now and again the privilege of standing upon some Pisgah height and wistfully gazing upon the promised land afar, or are we in the possession and enjoyment of the goodly land, "a land that flows with milk and honey?" *Are we still on the road,* or have we *arrived*? Are our religious thinking and experience up-to-date, or are we behind the spiritual times?

If I go into one of our assemblies of praise I find that we are still "tarrying at Jerusalem," waiting for "the Promise of the Father." We are busy invoking instead of receiving, busy asking rather than using. If I listen to the phraseology of the hymns I discover that the outlook of the soul is frequently pre-Pentecostal:—

Father, glorify Thy Son:
Answering His all-powerful prayer,
Send that Intercessor down,
Send that other Comforter!
Descend with all Thy gracious powers;
O come, great Spirit, come!

I think that if the Apostle Paul were to visibly enter our assembly when we are singing these strained and fervid supplications he would wonderingly and anxiously ask: "Did ye receive the Holy Ghost when ye believed?" He would wonder that men should plead for a Presence when the Presence Himself is pleading to be received! He would wonder that men should continue the strains of the exile when the native air is about their souls! When I listen to some of our prayers, and mark the pose and inclination of the soul, and note its uncertain longings, its timid askings, its trembling waiting for an event which has happened, its sighing for a gift that is already given, I can scarcely realize that the One with whom we are dealing is "a gracious willing Guest, where He can find one humble heart wherein to rest." The attitude is pre-Pentecostal; it is the language of the wilderness; it is not "one of the songs of Zion!"

But when I look a little more deeply at this mental temper, and investigate more closely the nature of its conception, I find that we are still more profoundly allied with the imperfect mood and inclination of the pre-Pentecostal day. Is it native to the Christian inheritance that we should so commonly conceive of the Spirit as an influence, a force, an energy, an atmosphere, an impersonal breath? I know the limitations of the human mind, and I know the fertile and helpful ministry of simile and symbol. I know how inclined we are to dwell in the realm of effects, and to express those very effects in the shrines of figurative speech. It is beautiful and true to speak of some gracious influence upon the soul by the imagery of a wind, or a fire, or of light, or of dew, or of rain. I say it is a beautiful and a helpful ministry; but if this be the predominant characteristic of our thinking we are pre-Pentecostal men and women, and we are self-deprived of the strength and glory of our larger and richer day. The all-encompassing glory of the Christian day is this—that we are dealing, not with an energy, but with a Person—not with "it," but with "Him!" Now, see our danger. We are living in a time when men are busy reducing all phenomena beneath the categories of definite law and order. No phenomenon is now regarded as a lawless vagrant, the sport of a sad or happy chance, wandering as chartered libertine through the mighty wastes of space. Everything pays obeisance to law. And so, too, in the realm of the spirit, we are busy eliminating chance and caprice; we are taking the tides of ambition, the gusts of passion, the movements of desire, and the kindlings of love, and we are reducing them to the dominion of sovereign law. We are seeing more and more clearly that things are not erratic and lawless just because they are spiritual and ethereal, and that "the law of the Spirit of life in Christ Jesus" is as constant as the laws that breathe in the material world. Well, all this is wise and good and inevitable. Only let us see to it that we do not so far bow to a tendency as to enthrone a law in place of a Companion, and exalt a force in place of a Counsellor and Friend. We shall lose unspeakably, and miss the fine fervour and flavour of Apostolic life, if our larger knowledge of law attenuates our fellowship with a Person, and our greater familiarity with forces impair our intimacy with the immediate heart of God. "A something not ourselves that makes for righteousness" may be a notable expression of scientific thought, but it is not the language of religion. "A something not ourselves that makes for righteousness," when translated into religious speech, becomes " a Friend that sticketh closer than a brother," and when translated into the New Testament evangel it becomes "the communion of the Holy Ghost." Our fellowship is not with a "something" but with a "Somebody," not with a force but with a Spirit, not with "it" but with "Him!"

It is just here, I think, that Keswick is contributing a vital emphasis to the thought of the modern Church. I do not identify myself with all the mental methods and instruments of Keswick. I think its Old Testament exegesis is often fanciful. I think its symbolisms are often forced and artificial. I think it has often laboured to erect doctrinal structures upon a

tabernacle-pin when it could have found a much more satis-
factory base. I think it has shown a little timidity in the application of its dynamic in the wider fields of social and national life. But even these are criticisms which are directed
more at yesterday than at the life and teaching of to-day. The
all-predominant teaching of Keswick is the personality of the
Holy Ghost, and the wonderful and glorious privilege of the
Christian believer to have holy and intimate companionship
with Him. They do not deal with an influence, they walk with
a Friend! There is nothing new in the teaching it is only the
recovery of an emphasis, with this further uniqueness, that
while so many of us are contented with the proclamation of
the fellowship they are busy in the enjoyment of it, and
about their lives there is a strength, and a serenity, and a
flavour, and a fragrance, which mark them off from the ha-
rassed, restless, feverish world they are seeking to redeem. I
miss this glaring contrast between the Church and the world!
The saved are too much like the unsaved; the physician is
labouring under the disease of his patient; there is no outstanding and commanding difference; we do not, with sufficient legibleness, bear God's name "in our foreheads." What
is the reason? Is it that we are not long enough in His company to receive the imprint of the fair and gracious seal? Is it
that we are having mental commerce with an "it" instead of
ceaseless communion with "Him?" I declare my own conviction that here is the secret of much of our impoverishment. We are living too much as men lived before the
Holy Ghost was given. We have not occupied the new and
far-stretching land of Christian privilege. We have not seized
upon our inheritance of august and holy companionship,
and, therefore, many of the gifts and graces and perfumes of
the Apostolic age are absent from our modern religious life.

You cannot, by fellowship with an energy, produce that
exquisite little flower called "heart's-ease," which was so pro-
lific and abounding in the life of the Apostle Paul. The
prophet of the Old Testament hints at the coming of the

flower in his illumined phrase, "He that believeth shall not make haste!" What a word for our own day! He shall not get excited, become fussy, or be thrown into panic! "He shall not make haste!" There shall be progress without much perspiration! There shall be strenuousness without strain! There shall be running without panting! "They shall run and not be weary, they shall walk and not faint." They shall be fed with "hidden manna." In the very midst of turbulence shall heart's-ease grow. "He that believeth shall not make haste."

O blessed life! the heart at rest
When all without tumultuous seems!

I say you cannot grow that flower in cooperation with an influence or a force, but only in the strength and grace of a glorious companionship. It is not the product of an energy: it is born of a communion. It is "peace in the Holy Ghost." Do you see much of this flower called "heart's-ease" about to-day? When the world gazes upon us, the professed disciples of the Master, does it see just a reflection of itself, its own wear and tear, its own strain and worry, or does it stoop to gaze upon a rare flower, and to wonder and to inquire about the soil in which it was grown? Is there anything about our speech and behaviour to suggest that "wear and tear" are counteracted by a secret renewal, the renewal of the Holy Spirit, "the inward man being renewed day by day?" Speaking for myself, I have to say that even when for a day I enter upon my inheritance, and realize the ineffable nearness of the great Companion-Spirit, the strain not only goes out of my mind and heart, but I feel the very wrinkles and care-lines being smoothed out of my face. If we were children of Pentecost, living up to our spiritual times, heart's-ease would bloom just within our gate, and the weary wayfarer would be stopped by its perfume, and would question us as to the secret and manner of its growth.

You cannot, by fellowship with a force, produce the exquisite grace of Apostolic tenderness. Have you ever studied the strength and softness of Apostolic tenderness? Why, their very rebukes and severities emerge from their tendernesses! Mark the tenor and order of this Apostolic counsel: "Full of goodness, filled with all knowledge, *able also to admonish!*" Do you see where admonition has to be born? Who is to be the monitor? One "filled with all knowledge!" Back still further! "Full of goodness!" Who would not be helped by admonition which came clothed in this tender bloom? But see again: "Admonishing one another in psalms and hymns and spiritual songs"; and even this singing monitor has first of all to "put on a heart of compassion!" All this tenderness is not the softness of weakness; it is the bloom of strength, and is born of the refining and chastening ministry of a great Companionship. We cannot live in the communion of the Holy Ghost without our unnecessary asperities being smoothed, away; the very power of the fellowship subdues them into tenderness. And, my brethren, there must never have been a time when it was more needful to ensure this tenderness than to-day. In these days of hard controversy we must beware of becoming hard. Men who become hard lose the power to inflict hard blows. The most tremendous antagonist is the man who is inherently tender. The only overwhelming anger is "the wrath of the Lamb." No, my brethren; we cannot fight without it! We cannot preach without it! You may perhaps remember how Andrew Bonar and Robert M'Cheyne were having one of their frequent walks together, talking over the ways of their ministry, when "M'Cheyne asked me," says Bonar, "what my last Sabbath's subject had been. It had been: 'The wicked shall be turned into hell.' On hearing this awful text, he asked: 'Were you able to preach it with tenderness?'" Shall we repeat Robert M'Cheyne's question to one another? When we speak on the destiny of the sinful, or on any one of the awful severities of the Word, are we "able to preach it with tenderness," with a melting heart, with secret tears? They say that M'Cheyne's severities were terrific, they were so tender! And I do not wonder at his tenderness, for he lived enfolded in the companionship of the Holy Ghost. He was ever holding converse with Him, and how could he become hard? "Oh," said his domestic servant; "oh! to hear Mr. M'Cheyne at prayers in the mornin'! It was as if he would never gi'e ower; he had sae muckle[3] to ask." How could he become hard, abiding in a Companionship which was forever communicating to him the very gentleness of God? You will not get that exquisite sensitiveness from a force; you will get it only from an intimate Friend. "Thy gentleness hath made me great":—

Tender Spirit, dwell with me,
I myself would tender be:
And with words that help and heal,
Would Thy life in mine reveal;
And with actions brotherly,
Speak my Lord's sincerity.

And let me add this further word. There is a certain compulsory impressiveness of character which attaches to profound spirituality, and which is commandingly present in those who walk in the fellowship of the Holy Ghost. I know not how to define it. It is a certain convincing aroma, self-witnessing, like the perfume of a flower. It is independent of mental equipment, and it makes no preference between a plenteous and a penurious estate. It works without the aid of speech because it is the effluence of a silent and secret communion. It begins to minister before you preach; it continues its ministry when the sermon is ended. It is endowed with marvellous powers of compulsion, and it sways the lives of others when mere words would miserably fail. The pitman

---

3   muckle: a large number or amount or extent

away yonder in the county of Durham felt the strength of this mystic constraint when he said of his old vicar, "You have only to shake that man's hand to feel that he is full of the Holy Ghost!" And his fellow in toil, an agricultural labourer in a not distant village, was bowing beneath the same persuasion when, speaking of another, he said, "I never saw that man cross the common, sir, without being the better for it!" What is it, this mysterious influence? It is this: "He that believeth on Me, as the Scripture hath said, out of his belly shall flow rivers of living water. But this spake He of the Spirit, which they that believed in Him were to receive, for the Spirit was not yet given, because Jesus was not yet glorified." Then it was not the vicar whom the pitman felt, but the vicar's great Companion; it was not the man who crossed the common, but the man's inseparable Guest and Friend. My brethren, Jesus is now glorified! The Holy Ghost has been given! We, too, may cross our common, and by the very crossing make men better: for in the prayerful fostering of a conscious friendship with Him the "rivers of living water" will flow from you and me.

I have been leading you among the rudiments of our religious faith and life. I make no apology. "We must need to learn the things we have known the longest." Why should a man apologize for leading his fellows to the running waters and the bracing air of the open moor? We are infinitely richer than we dream. Ours is the Pentecostal inheritance. Let us assume the Pentecostal attitude of zealous and hungry reception. Above all, let us cultivate a sensitive intimacy with the Holy Spirit Let us listen to Him, let us talk to Him, let us consult Him in all the changing seasons of the changing days, and let us greedily receive His proffered gifts of enlightenment and grace. He will be our all-sufficiency, and we shall move about in the enduement of Pentecostal power.

A little while ago I had a day-dream, one of those subjective visions which sometimes visit the mind in seasons of wakeful meditation and serious thought I was in my study in the early morning, before the day's work was begun, and I was somewhat sadly contemplating the comparative weakness of my ministry and the many shortcomings in my personal life. And while I pondered, with closed eyes, I became aware of a Presence before whom my spirit bowed in trembling awe. He lifted my garments, and I saw that they were badly stained. He went away, and came again, and again He lifted my robes, and began to remove the stains, and I saw that He was using the ministry of blood. And then He touched my lips, and they became pure as the lips of a little child. And then He anointed mine eyes with eye-salve, and I knew He was giving sight to the blind. Then He breathed upon my brow, and my depression passed away like a morning cloud. And I wondered what next my august Companion would do, and with the eyes and ears of my spirit I watched and listened. Then He took a pen, and putting it into my hand He said, "Write, for I will take of the things of Christ and show them unto thee." And I turned to my desk and I wrote in the communion of the Holy Ghost.

CHAPTER 6

The Disciple's Rest

"Come unto Me all ye that labour and are heavy laden and I will give you rest. Take My yoke upon you and learn of Me, for I am meek and lowly in heart, and ye shall find rest unto your souls" — Matthew 11:28-29

"I WILL give you rest." Give! This kind of rest is always a gift; it is never earned. It is not the emolument of toil; it is the dowry of grace. It is not the prize of endeavour, its birth precedes endeavour, and is indeed the spring and secret of it. It is not the perquisite of culture, for between it and culture there is no necessary and inevitable communion. It broods in strange and illiterate places, untouched by scholastic and academic refinement, but it abides also in cultured souls which have been chastened by the manifold ministry of the schools. It is not a work, but a fruit; not the product of organization, but the sure and silent issue of a relationship. "Come unto Me,... and I will give you rest."

But even the gift of rest does not disclose its unutterable contents in a day. It is an immediate gift, but it is also a continuous discovery. "Learn of Me,... and ye shall find rest." Part of "the things which God hath prepared for them that love Him" lie in this wealthy gift of rest, and it is one of the

frequent and delightful surprises of grace that we should re-
peatedly come upon new and unexpected veins of ore in
this deep mine of "the peace of God which passeth all understanding." I say that the rest of the Lord is an immediate
gift and a perpetual discovery. "Come unto Me,... and I will
give you rest." "Learn of Me... and ye shall find rest unto
your souls."

And so I am to speak to you of the riches of the Christian rest. Do you feel it to be an irrelevant note, an inappropriate theme, in the march and warfare of our times? Surely,
we need to speak of battle-fields rather than of green pastures, and to hear the nerving call to struggle and duty rather
than the soft and gentle wooings that call to rest! Our times
demand the warrior's bugle-peal, and not the shepherd's pipe
of peace! Ah, but, brethren, in this warfare the trumpeter himself is shorn of inspiration unless he have the gift of rest,
and the warrior himself is rendered impotent unless he be
possessed by the secret of the heavenly peace. The restless
trumpeter ministers no thrill, and the perturbed warrior lacks
the very genius of conquest. I know the feverish motions of
our time, the restlessness of fruitless desire, the disturbing
forebodings of anxiety, the busy-ness of the devil, the
sleepless and perspiring activity of Mammon, the rush to be
rich, the race to be happy, the craving for sensation, the immense impetus and speed characterizing every interest in our
varied life, and added to all, the precipitate shedding of hoary
forms and vestures, and the re-clothing of the thoughts of
men in modern and more congenial attire. I know the general restlessness, the heated and consuming haste, and know-
ing them I proclaim that the secret of a successful antagonism must be sought in the profound restfulness of the
Church. I do not wonder at the restlessness of the world, but
I stand amazed at the restlessness of the Saviour's Church!
We are encountering restlessness by restlessness, and on
many sides we are suffering defeat. The antagonist ought to
be of quite another order. The contendents must be restful-

ness versus rest, and the odds will be overwhelmingly on our side. Let me pause to make a few distinctions in order that my argument may not be misunderstood. We must distinguish between indolent passivity and active restfulness. I am not pleading for enervating ease, but for enabling and inspiring rest. Ease is an opiate; rest is a stimulant, say, rather a nutriment. Ease is the enemy of strength; rest is its hidden resource. I do not stand here, therefore, as the advocate of the couch, but as the advocate of restful and therefore invincible movement. Our scientists distinguish between motion and energy, and I could wish that some similar distinction might be transferred to the sphere of the Church. All activity is not influential. All speech is not persuasive. All supplication is not effective. The secret of effective supplication is a quiet faith. The secret of effective speech is a hidden assurance. The secret of triumphant warfare is a permanent peace. The essential and operative element in all fruitful activity is a deep and abiding rest. We must fight the prevalent restlessness by a sovereign peace. "Come unto Me,... and I will give you rest."

Now, my brethren, I confess I miss this essential in the modern Church. How think you? Is the Church of our day characterized by that wealthy peace and rest which ought to be the portion of all saved, forgiven and sanctified men and women? I confess that peace and rest are about the last grace I think about when I gaze upon the modern Church! The care-lines, and the wrinkles of worry and anxiety and uncertainty, and a general air of restlessness, seem to me almost as prevalent upon the countenance of the Church as upon the face of the world. The Church is not conspicuous by the smoothness of its brow! Everywhere I detect a certain strain, a certain fussy precipitancy, a certain trembling activity, a certain emasculating care. We look like men and women who are carrying more than we can bear, and, who are attempting tasks that are quite beyond our strength. If I listen to our prevailing vocabulary, and note the words that are most in evidence, my impression of the general rest-lessness is only confirmed. The vocabulary is scriptural enough so far as it goes, but the real fertilizing terms are too much obscured or ignored. The great, hot, dry words in the terminology are manifest enough: strive, fight, wrestle, oppose, work, war, do, endeavour; but those gracious, energizing words, lying there with the soft dews upon them: grace, rest, joy, quietness, assurance, these deep, generic words are not sufficiently honoured in our modern speech. I am calling for the resurrection of these domestic terms in order that the military terms may be revived. I am calling to peace for the sake of warfare. I am calling to rest for the sake of labour. I plead for a little more mysticism for the sake of our enthusiasms. I proclaim the sacredness and necessity of the cloister in the soul, the necessity of a chamber of peace, a centre of calmness, a "heart at rest, when all without tumultuous seems." Rest is the secret of conquest, and it is to the Church therefore, and not to the world, that I primarily offer this evangel today: "Come unto Me, all ye that labour and are heavy laden, and I will give you rest."

Now, when I look around upon the strained and wrinkled Church, moving often in the pallor of fear and uncertainty when she ought to exult in the pink of strength and assurance, I am impressed with certain primary lacks in her equipment. The strain frequently comes at the hill; not always so, perhaps not even commonly so, for perhaps it is true both of men and of Churches that the strain is not so much felt in the sharp and passing crisis as in the dull and jogging commonplace. Perhaps there is more strain in the prolonged drudgery than in the sudden calamity. The dead level may try us more than the hill! "Because they have no changes they fear not God." But come the strain how it may, all strain is suggestive of inadequate resources; and the wrinkled, restless, careworn face of the Church makes it abundantly evident that the Church is not entering into the fullness of "the inheritance of the saints in light." What does the

Church require if her strain and her paralyzing restlessness are to be removed? She needs a more restful realization of her Lord's Presence. My brethren, we fight too much as soldiers whose leader is out of the field. We work too much as though our Exemplar were a dead Nazarene, instead of a living and immediate friend. We tear about with the aimless, pathetic wanderings of little chicks when the mother-bird is away. And so our life is strained and restless and uninspired, when it might be filled with a big and bracing contentment. We need the stimulating consciousness of a great and ever-present Companionship. We know the stimulus of lofty companionship in other spheres and in smaller communions. We know the influence of Stevenson's companionship upon Mr. Barrie and Mr. Crockett. That companionship acted like a second literary conscience, restraining all careless and hasty work, but it also acted as an unfailing inspiration, quickening the very tissues of their minds and souls. It was a companionship that was not only like a great white throne of literary judgment, but a throne out of which there flowed, as there does out of every engaging personality, a river of water of life, vitalizing all who hold communion with it. But when we lift up the relationship, and contemplate the great communion which we are all privileged to share in the companionship of the Lord, all similes tire and fall limp and ineffective, and leave the glory unexpressed! A restful realization of the Lord's companionship! That has been the characteristic of all men whose religious activity has been forceful, influential and fertile in the purposes of the kingdom. At the very heart of all their labours, in the very centre of their stormiest days, there is a sphere of sure and restful intimacy with the Lord. You know how close and intimate and calm such intimacy can be. I think of Samuel Rutherford. I think of the love-language which he uses in his communion with the Lord. Only the Song of Solomon can supply him with suitable expressions of holy passion wherewith to tell the story of his soul's devotion. When I read some of his words I almost feel as though I were eavesdropping, and had overheard two lovers in their gentle and wooing speech. It is a fashion of language not congenial to our time, but that is only because in our day we have almost ceased to cultivate the affections, and confine our education to the culture of the intellect and the conscience. "We now make critics, not lovers," and the love-impassioned speech of Samuel Rutherford sounds to us like an alien tongue. Samuel Rutherford had a sweet and restful intimacy with his Lord, and therefore he was never idle, and never feared the coming day. I think of Jonathan Edwards, a man of greatly differing type from Samuel Rutherford, but also a man of multitudinous labours and of fearless persistence, and whose activities rested upon a sublime repose in the abiding sense of the reality and presence of his Lord. His latest biographer declares that he had "an immediate vision of the spiritual universe as the reality of realities," that "in exploring its recesses and in pondering its relations he did so as native and to the manner born," and that perhaps next to the Apostle John he exercised the surest and most intimate familiarity with things unseen. I think of David Hill, and I am conscious of the sweet and gracious perfume which was ever rising from his full and ever-moving life. At the heart of this busy worker was the restful lover; he moved about in assured and certain warfare because his soul was ever feasting in love-companionship with his Lord. I like this sentence of his: "What a thrill it gives me to meet with one who has fallen in love with Jesus!" Ah, but that is the speech of a lover, who is himself in love with the Lord. It is the thrill of sympathetic vibrations; it is the thrill of one who is already in love with the lover, and who delights to see the Lover come to His own. David Hill's sort of warfare finds its explanation in the lover's thrill, and in the lover's thrill has its secret in the lover's rest. But why should I keep upon these high planes of renowned and prominent personalities? Get a man who is restfully intimate with his Lord, and you have a man whose force is tremendous! Such men move in apparent ease, but it is the ease that is linked with the infinite, it is the very rest of God.

They may be engaged in apparent trifles, but even in the doing of the trifles there emerges the health-giving currents of the Kingdom of God. Listen to James Smetham: "I was at the leaders' meeting last night. There was the superintendent. There were a gardener, a baker, a cheese-monger, a postman and myself. We sat till near to P. M. Now what were the topics? When is the juvenile missionary meeting to be? When the society tea-meeting? How best to distribute the poor money, etc.?" Here were these unknown and unlettered men, engaged in apparently trivial business, but resting in the Lord, and pouring forth from their rest-possessed souls spiritual energy which to James Smetham is like "healthy air," and "send me home," he says, "as last night, cured to the core, so fresh, so calm, so delivered from all my fears and troubles." The man who is sure and restful in the conscious companionship of his Lord has about him the strainlessness and inevitableness of the ocean tide, and gives off bracing influence like God's fresh and wondrous sea. "Then had Thy peace been like a river, and Thy righteousness like the waves of the sea." Let us become restfully sure of God, and we shall meet the battalions of the evil one unstrained and undismayed. "Hold the fort, for I am coming!" The doctrine is pernicious, and fills the life with strain, and fear, and uncertainty! "For I am coming!" "The Lord of Hosts is with us; the God of Jacob is our refuge." Let the Church rest in her Lord, and she will become terrible as an army with banners. "Come unto Me,... and I will give you rest."

What does the Church need if her strain and her wrinkles are to be removed? She needs a more restful realization of the wealth and power of her allies. We too often face our foes with the shiver of fear, and with the pallor of expected defeat We too often manifest the symptoms of panic, instead of marching out in orderly array with the restful assurance of conquest. The hosts of evil are even now organizing their forces in threatening and terrific mass. Are our wrinkles increasing? Is our fear intensifying our strain, and are we possessed by a great uncertainty? Why, brethren, if we were conscious of our resources, and recognized our cooperative allies, we should more frequently put the Doxology at the beginning of our programmes, and our hearts would sing of victory even before the conflict began! It is all a matter of being more restfully conscious of the allies that fight on our side. Paul was a great hand at numbering up his friends, and so great was the company that he always felt his side was overwhelming! He periodically reviews the cooperative forces, and invariably marches on with a more impassioned Doxology. Think of our resources in grace. You cannot turn to any of the epistles of the great Apostle without feeling how immense and immediate is his conception of his helpmeets in grace. Grace runs through all his arguments. It is allied with all his counsel. It bathes all his ethical ideals. It flows like a river close by the highway of his life, winding with all his windings, and remaining in inseparable companionship. But my figure is altogether ineffective. Paul's conception of life was not that of road and river—the common highway of duty with its associated refreshment of grace. Grace was to Paul an all-enveloping atmosphere, a defensive and oxygenating air, which braced and nourished his own spirit, and wasted and consumed his foes. "The abundant grace!" "The riches of the grace!" "The exceeding riches of His grace!" can never recall Paul's conception of grace without thinking of broad, full rivers when the snows have melted on the heights, of brimming springtides, and of overwhelming and submerging floods. "Where sin abounded grace did much more abound!" And, brethren, these glorious resources of grace are ours, our allies in the work, and march, and conflict of our times. Don't you think that if she realized them, the Church would lose her wrinkles and her strain, and would move in the strength and the assurance of a glorious rest? I like that dream of Josephine Butler's, when her life passed into deep shadow, amid many frowning and threatening besetments: "I thought I was lying flat, with a restful feeling, on a smooth, still sea, a boundless ocean, with no limit or shore on any side. It was strong and held me up, and there was light and sunshine all around me. And I heard a voice say, 'Such is the grace of God!'" Let the Church even dimly realize the force of this tremendous ally, and she will move with a strength and quietness which will give her the secret of perpetual conquest.

And think of our allies in circumstances! Devilry has not the unimpeded run of the field. Somewhere in the field, let me rather say everywhere in the field, there is hidden the Divine Antagonist. The apparent is not the fundamental. The immediate trend does not represent the final issue. The roystering adversary runs up against Almighty God, and all his feverish schemes are turned agley. It is marvellous to watch the terrific twist given to circumstances by the compulsion of an unseen and mysterious hand. "The things that happened unto me have turned out rather unto the progress of the Gospel." So sings the Apostle Paul, and the experience has become so familiar to him that now, in the days of his great besetments, he always quietly and confidently awaits the action of the mighty, secret pressure which changes the temporary misfortune into permanent advantage. "I know that even this shall turn to my salvation through your prayer and the supply of the Spirit of Christ Jesus." How can a man with that persuasion be shaken with panic? How can he fight and labour in any spirit but the restful optimism of a triumphant hope? Do not let us quake before circumstances, or lapse into unbelieving restlessness and strain. The secret of circumstance belongeth unto God. The unseen drift is with us. The nature of things is on our side. "Thou shalt be in league with the stones of the field." The universal yearning of the material world corroborates the purpose of our advance. "The whole creation groaneth and travaileth" in profoundest sympathy with the evolution and "manifestation of the children of God." The planet itself is pledged against the devil. "The stars in their courses fought against Sisera." "They that be with us are more than they that be against us." "And Elijah prayed, and said, Lord, I pray Thee, open his eyes that he may see. And the Lord opened the eyes of the young man, and he saw; and, behold, the mountain was full of horses and chariots of fire." Our allies are everywhere and anywhere! Why should our faces be strained? Why should we toil in restless fear? Why should the Church be wrinkled like the world? "Christ loved the Church, and gave Himself for it,... that He might present it to Himself a glorious Church, not having spot, or wrinkle, or any such thing."

And let me add one closing word. I think the Church needs a more restful disposition in the ministry of prayer. I am amazed at the want of restfulness in our communion with the Lord! I do not speak of our unnecessary loudness, but of the feverish uncertainty, the strained and painful clutch and cleaving, the perspiring pleading which is half- suggestive of unbelief. Let me say it in great reverence, and not in a spirit of idle and careless criticism, when I listen to some prayers I find it difficult to realize that we are speaking to the One who said, "Behold, I stand at the door and knock; if any man hear My voice, and open the door, I will come in to him, and sup with him, and he with Me." Our strained and restless prayers do not suggest the quiet opening of a door, they rather suggest a frenzied and fearful prisoner, hallooing to a God who has turned His back upon our door, and the sound of whose retreating footsteps is lessening in the far-away. We need a firmer and quieter assurance while we pray. Yes, even in our supplications it is needful to "rest in the Lord." Perhaps it would be a good thing for many of us in our praying seasons if we were to say less and to listen more. "I will hear what God the Lord will speak." Listening might bring restfulness where speech would only inflame us. It is not an insignificant thing that the marginal rendering of that lovely phrase, "Rest in the Lord," is just this, "Be silent unto the Lord!" Perhaps we need a little more of the Quaker silence and receptiveness, and a little less of heated speech and aggression. At any rate, we must get the doubt-wrinkles out of our prayers, and in our speech with God we must manifest the assurance of a calm and fruitful faith.

I call you then to rest! Nay, the Master Himself is the caller: "Come unto Me," thou strained and care-worn Church, "Come unto Me," and I will distinguish thee from the world, for "I will give thee rest."

Drop Thy still dews of quietness,
 Till all our strivings cease;
Take from our souls the strain and stress,
 And let our ordered lives confess
The beauty of Thy peace.

CHAPTER 7

The Disciple's Vision

"But in the latter days it shall come to pass" — *Micah 4:1*

"BUT in the latter days it shall come to pass... ." The prophet lifts his eyes away to the latter days to gain refreshment in his present toil. He feasts his soul upon the golden age which is to be, in order that he may nerve himself in his immediate service. Without the anticipation of a golden age he would lose his buoyantly, and the spirit of endeavour would go out of his work. Our visions always determine the quality of our tasks. Our dominant thought regulates our activities. What pattern any I working by? What golden age have I in my mind? What do I see as the possible consummation of my labours? I may be keenly conscious of what I am working at, but what am I working for? What do I see in the latter days? There is your child at home. You are ministering to him in your daily attention and service. What is your pattern in the mind? How do you see him in the long run? How looks he in your mind's eye? What sort of a man do you see in your boy? How would you fill up this imperfect phrase concerning him "In the latter days it shall come to pass...?" Have you ever painted his possibilities? If you have no clear golden age for the boy your training will be uncertain, your discipline will be a guesswork and a chance. You must come to your child with a vision of the man you would like him to be, and the vision will shape and control all your ministries. Our visions are our dies, quietly, ceaselessly pressing against the plastic material of the lives for which we labour. Our vision of possibilities helps to shape the actuality.

There is the scholar in the school. When a teacher goes to his class, be it a class of boys or girls, what kind of men and women has he in his eye? Surely we do not go to work among our children in blind and good-humoured chance? We are the architects and builders of their characters, and we must have some completed conception even before we begin our work. I suppose the architect sees the finished building in his eye even before he takes a pencil in his hand, and certainly long before the pick and the spade touch the virgin soil. It is built up in imagination before he cuts the first sod. It must not be otherwise with our children in the schools. Again I say, we must be able to complete the unfinished phrase: "In the latter days it shall come to pass..." We must deliberately fill in the blank, and see clearly the consummation at which we aim. That boy who gives the teacher so much trouble; restless, indifferent, bursting with animal vitality, how is he depicted as man in your chamber of imagery? Do you only see him as he is? Little, then, will be your influence to make him what he might be. You must see a golden age for the boy, a splendid prime, and so every moment your ardent vision will be operating to realize itself in the unpromising material of the present.

Let me assume that your work is among the outcasts. When you go to court and alley, or to the elegant house in the favoured suburb, and find men and women sunk in animalism, trailing the robes of human dignity in unnameable mire, how do you see them with the eyes of the soul? "In the latter days it shall come to pass...." What? To the eye of sense they are filthy, offensive, repellent. What like are their faces, and what sort of robes do they wear in the vision of the soul? Do we address the beast as the gentleman-to-be? Are we dealing with the "might-be" or only with the thing that is? Sir Titus Salt was pacing the docks at Liverpool and saw great quantities of dirty, waste material lying in unregarded heaps. He looked at the un-promising substance, and in his mind's eye saw finished fab-rics and warm and welcome garments; and ere long the power of the imagination devised ministries for converting the outcast stuff into refined and finished robes. We must look at all our waste material in human life and see the vision of the "might-be." I took out a little sentence the other day from a book I was reading, a sentence which fell from the lips of one of the un-fortunate women who so greatly add to the sins of our great cities. Some man had done her a courtesy, spoken to her in kindly tone and manner, and surprised and thrilled her cold and careless heart. "He raised his hat to me as if I were a lady!" The man had addressed her as she might be, and the buried dignity within her rose to the call. He spoke to her in the lan-guage of the golden age, and she lifted her eyes to the vision revealed.

Surely this was the Master's way! He is always calling the thing that is by the name of its "might-be." "Thou art Simon," a mere hearer; "Thou shalt be called Peter," a rock. To the woman of sin, the outcast child of the city, He addressed the gracious word "daughter," and spoke to her as if she were al-ready a child of the golden age; her weary heart leaped to the welcome speech. And so we have got to come to our work with visions of the latter days, glimpses of the "might-be," pic-tures of the golden age, or the cheap and tinselled present will never be enriched. Take your child, your scholar, or the outcast man in the court, or the degraded man in the villa, and get well into your mind and heart a vision of all they might be. Spend time over it. Work it out line upon line. Make it superlatively beautiful and noble. Then, with that vision of the later day, ad-dress yourself to the present day; and your vision will domi-nate your very muscles, and every movement of service will be a minister of elevation and refinement.

I am not surprised, therefore, that all great reformers and all men and women who have profoundly influenced the life and thought of their day have been visionaries, having a clear sight of things as they might be, feeling the cheery glow of the light and heat of the golden age. Abraham, amid the idolatrous cities of his own day, had a vision of the latter days, and, while labouring in the present, "looked for the city which hath foundations whose builder and maker is God." The Apostle John, in the Island of Patmos, while impressed with the iniquity of Rome seated on her seven hills, and drunk with the blood of saints, saw through the Rome that was to the Rome that might be, "The Holy City, the new Jerusalem, coming down from God out of heaven, made ready as a bride adorned for husband." And so has it been through all the changing centuries right down to our own time. In my own city of Birmingham forty years ago, when North and South America were locked in bloody strife, and it seemed as though the future were pregnant with nothing but quarrel and discord, John Bright lifted the eyes of his countrymen to the glory of the latter days, and unfolded to them the radiant colours of the golden age: "It may be but a vision, but I will cherish it; I see one vast federation stretch from the frozen north in unbroken line to the glowing south, and from the wild billows of the Atlantic westward to the calmer waters of the Pacific main. And I see one people and one language, and one law and one faith, and over all that white continent the home of freedom and a refuge for the oppressed of every race and every clime."

And so the prophet Micah, in a book that is crowded with severity and denunciation and indictment, and noisy with thunder and frightful in its lightning, still lets us hear the music of the latter days, and permits us to contemplate the vision of the golden age in which he travailed and toiled: "In the latter days it shall come to pass... ." What are the characteristics of the golden age to which the prophet was looking with hungry and aspiring spirit? "The mountain of the Lord's house shall be established in the top of the mountains, and it shall be exalted above the hills." Then in the golden age emphasis is to be given to the spiritual. The mountain of the Lord's house is to be established at the top of the mountain. I think of Durham city as an emblem of the prophet's thought. Away in the lower reaches of the city there is the river, on which boats are plying for pleasure and recreation. A little higher up on the slopes are the places of business, the ways and byways of trade. A little higher there is the castle hill, on which the turretted tower presents its imposing front; but on a higher summit, commanding all and overlooking all, there rises and towers aloft the majesty of the glorious old cathedral. Let me interpret the emblem. The river is typical of pleasure, the ways of business are representatives of money, the castle is the symbol of armaments, the cathedral is significant of God. In the latter days the spiritual is to have emphasis above pleasure, money, armaments. In whatever prominence these may be seen, they are all to be subordinate to the reverence and worship of God. Military prowess and money- making and pleasure-seeking are to be put in their own place, and not to be permitted to leave it. First things first I "In the beginning God." This is the first characteristic of the golden age.

"And many nations shall come and say: Come and let us go up to the mountain of the Lord and to the house of the God of Jacob, and He will teach us His ways, and we will walk in His paths." Then the second characteristic of the golden age is that people are to find their confluence and unity in common worship. The brotherhood is to be discovered in spiritual communion. We are not to find profound community upon the river of pleasure or in the ways of business or in the armaments of the castle. These are never permanently cohesive. Pleasure is more frequently divisive than cohesive. At the present time we have abundant evidence that commerce may be a severing ministry among the peoples of the earth. And certainly we do not find union in common armaments. Two nations may fight side by side to-day, and may confront each other tomorrow. No, it is in the mountain of the Lord's house the peoples will discover their unity and kinship. It is in the common worship of the one Lord, in united adoration of the God revealed in Christ, that our brotherhood will be unburied, and we shall realize how rich is our oneness in Him.

"And they shall beat their swords into ploughshares, and their spears into pruning hooks." Then the third characteristic of the golden age is to be the conversion of merely destructive force into positive and constructive ministries. No energy is to be destroyed: it is all to be transfigured. The sword is to become a ploughshare; the weapon of destruction an implement of culture. I saw a picture the other day which was intended to represent the re-enshrinement of peace. A cannon had dropped from its battered carriage and was lying in the meadow, rusting away to ruin. A lamb was feeding at its very mouth, and round it on every side the flowers were growing. But really that is not a picture of the golden age. The cannon is not to rust, it is to be converted, its strength is to be transfigured. After the Franco-German war many of the cannon balls were re-made into church bells. One of our manufacturers in Birmingham told me only a week ago that he was busy turning the empty cases of the shells used in the recent war into dinner gongs! That is the suggestion we seek in the golden age: all destructive forces are to be changed into helpful ministries. Tongues that speak nothing but malice are to be turned into instructors of wisdom. Passions that are working havoc and ruin are to be made the nourishers of fine endeavour and holy work. All men's gifts and powers, and all material forces, are to be used in the employment of the kingdom of God.

"They shall sit every man under his vine and under his fig-tree." That savours of Bournville! Yes, and Bournville is in the prophetic line, and has got something of the light and colour of the golden age. There is to be a distribution of comforts. Life's monotony is to be broken up. Sweet and winsome things are to be brought into the common life. Dinginess and want are both to be banished. There is to be a little beauty for everybody, something of the vine and the fig-tree. There is to be a little ease for everybody, time to sit down and rest. To every mortal man there is to be given a little treasure, a little leisure and a little pleasure. "And none shall make them afraid." And they are not only to have comfort but the added glory of peace. The gift of the vine and fig-tree would be nothing if peace remained an exile. There are many people who have both the vine and the fig-tree, but their life is haunted and disturbed by fears. In the golden age peace is to be the attendant of comfort, and both are to be guests in every man's dwelling.

And now mark the beautiful final touches in this prophet's dream: "I will assemble her that halteth, and I will gather her that is driven out, and her that is afflicted." They are all to be found in God's family. "Her that halteth," the child of "ifs" and "buts" and fears and indecision, she shall lose her halting and obtain a firm and confident step. "And her that is driven out," the child of exile, the self-banished son or daughter, the outcast by reason of sin; they shall all be home again! 'He gathereth together the outcasts." And along with these there is to come "her that is afflicted," the child of sorrows. The day of grief is to be ended, morning shall be the thing of the preparatory day which is over; "He shall wipe away all tears from their eyes, and sorrow and sighing shall flee away."

MORE FROM

C.C.R. Publishing

That Christ May Have Preeminence

Various Authors:

Isaac Ambrose, Samuel Davies, Thomas Watson, Octavius Winslow, Jonathan Edwards, Richard Sibbes, John Flavel and Thomas Chalmers

242 pages | ISBN: 978-1484998465

The Anxious Inquirer After Salvation, Directed And Encouraged
Author: John Angell James - 1834
129 pages | ISBN: 978-1-4960-1437-5